FINANCIAL CRIME INVESTIGATION

DR. KELLY MUA KINGSLY

ISBN 978-1-64114-340-0 (hardcover)
ISBN 978-1-64114-339-4 (digital)

Christian Faith Publishing, Inc.
832 Park Avenue
Meadville, PA 16335
www.christianfaithpublishing.com

Printed in the United States of America

CONTENTS

Preface..5
Foreword...7

Chapter 1. Financial Crime Overview, Commonalities,
     and Convergence 9
     Financial Crime Overview..............................9
     Defining Financial Crime and Its Permutations........10
     Scope of Financial/White-Collar Crime 12
     Technology Changes the Complexion of
       Financial Crime 13
     Globalization of Financial Crime............................14
     Financial/White-Collar Crime: An Evolving
       Concept..15
     Modern Conceptualizations of White-Collar Crime..20
     Commonalities of All Financial Crimes...................26
     Capitalizing On the "Commonalities" and
       Exploring "Convergence"....................31
     Consequences of White-Collar Crime 32

Chapter 2. Types of Financial Crimes 38
     Introduction...38
     Fraud Crime...39
     Occupational Fraud.....................................45
     Theft Crime 46
     Manipulation Crime 49
     Corruption Crime.......................................54
     Reflection Menu...58

Chapter 3. Why People Commit Financial Crimes...............59
     Introduction...59
     The Fraudsters 60

The Fraud Triangle and Diamond.............................63
Indicators of Financial Crimes Activities...................70
Reflection Menu...73

Chapter 4. Investigative Techniques in Financial Crimes 76
Investigative Techniques 76
Other Investigative Techniques..............................82
A Model for Investigations of Employee Fraud.........89

Chapter 5. Money Laundering 107
Introduction...107
The Money Laundering Process.............................107
Money Laundering Business...................................111
Favourite Businesses for Hiding or Laundering
    Money 112
AML and Forensic Accounting Investigation...........119
Potential Red Flags...121
Combating Money Laundering 124
Impact of Money Laundering.................................133
Reflection Menu..136

Chapter 6. Organized Financial Crimes....................................137
Introduction...137
Corporate Organization and Crimes 138
Criminogenic Organizational Structures.................143
Corporate Executives and Criminal Liability 146
Controlling Organizational Crime 149
Examples of Organized Financial Crime.................154
Agencies Involved in the Fighting Tax and
    Other Financial Crimes..................................158

Chapter 7. Tracing Illicit Transactions 162
Introduction...162
Direct Methods of Tracing Financial Transactions ...166
Indirect Methods of Tracing Financial Transactions .180

Appendix A: Answer to End-of-Book Questions 203

PREFACE

The most insidious threat to our way of life the markets and economy is financial crime. Having been as all citizens of the international community the victim of financial crime for me it is especially relevant for my dear friend and colleague (Dr. Kelly Mua Kingsly) to have crafted such an expertly written work. As most recently the great recession demonstrated to many around the world, financial crime is a serious concern for both the markets as well as the citizens of all nations. The Great Recession showed that financial crime is a prolific issue that affects every individual of the community. Regardless of investments in real estate or securities, as Bernie Madoff made this painfully clear to many of the most savvy investors on Wall Street bilking billions from investors, many lost their entire life savings and literally have no recourse to seek reparations; while due to other shady and or unethical practices, many more lost their greatest investment, the equity in their homes.

The fact that these crimes affect every member of society regardless of class, occupation, or status inevitably causes the reader to pause and contemplate the sheer depth and scope financial crimes reap on one's community. Further, this book addresses the disparity of perception between how "violent" crime and financial or "white collar" crime are perceived. Putting the focus squarely on how while violent crime often only affects an individual or small group and comparing how financial crimes affect not only markets and whole nations but also the entire global community. It became clear to me as I read and reread this enthralling and even at times humorous work that what it really comes down to is the ethics of business, how the atmosphere and pressure of business puts everything on a company's bottom line without regard for the greater economic consequences to the nation or international community.

My dear friend and colleague Asifa Baig of the Prudential Government of Ontario recently wrote, "The idea that business has no greater responsibility to the community is economic suicide... where is businesses responsibility to their communities?" She went on to coin a phrase (ROH) or "Return On Humanity is a concept that should be added to all companies balance sheets." Additionally, what makes financial crimes so insidious is the many varieties through which it manifests. Just last year, when working with the retired Minister of Finance for Ukraine, Volodymyr Ryaboshlyk, PhD, a "Prince" circumvented me and contacted him directly wanting to "meet in secret" and "exchange untraceable cash" to provide seed funding for an upcoming project. In the above example, the quoted phrases raised red flags for all involved and caused serious concerns not only for the likely illegal origins of possible funds but also for my friend and colleague's personal safety should such a meeting be arranged.

This expertly written text addresses these concerns empowering even the casual reader with a deep knowledge of financial crime investigation. Whether you are interested in seeking a position in financial crime investigation for a ministry or regulatory authority, an investor looking for clarity, or simply a curious citizen activist looking to make a difference locally, this book is for you professional policy writers, scholars, students, and for all who seek the fear of God and wellbeing of humanity.

Lee Common
Founder, Creative Movement in Sovereign
Wealth and Sovereign Wealth US

FOREWORD

Financial crimes through the rapid growth in information and communication technology have taken a deep leap. It is a concept we talk about, we complain about, something whose negative impact we recognize, but our level for tolerance for this crime is amazing. The effective investigation and prosecution of fraud and other white-collar crimes remains as difficult today as it was in 1948 when the Metropolitan and City of London Police Company Fraud Department was set up to cope with the increase in fraud cases that was apparent after the Second World War "Perry novy."

Financial crime over the last thirty years has increasingly posed great concern to governments throughout the world. It is today widely recognised that the prevalence of economically motivated crime in many societies is a substantial threat to the development of economies and their stability. Financial crimes are a form of theft/larceny that occur when a person or entity takes money or property or uses them in an illicit manner with the intent to gain a benefit from it. This book will introduce the reader to the forms of financial crimes, such as bribery, forgery, credit card fraud, embezzlement and money laundering, tax evasion, organized financial crimes, transnational financial crimes, and terrorist financing.

The judiciary is actively involved in the fight of this rather challenging concern that accounts for the dowdrain in the development process of emerging nations. The role of the police in this struggle cannot be over emphasized. However, if it takes two to tango, we shall understand this is not only a concern for the legal and judicial department alone. When we start talking of financial crime investigation, it means there is a wrong doing or alleged wrong doing, which the legal process will sure establish and punish the culprit.

Understanding the challenge from this prism, it is a consequence of societal breakdown that has led to this practice. If we must seek reedy; it is imperative we as a people start by taking responsibility in what we have done to perpetrate this act. It is only by taking responsibility for our action or inaction that we shall be able to help the institutions in place to curb this crime during investigation.

These pieces seek to throw light on salient topical issues relating to the concept and impediments of financial crime investigation.

As you read through this book, the author, Dr. Kelly Mua Kingsly, has crafted meticulously his work to help you understand the following:

- Identify the primary components of financial crime;
- identify the basics of financial crime investigation;
- describe how accounting principles relate to financial crime investigation;
- describe how criminal law and regulations relate to economic crime investigation;
- discuss the role of technology in the etiology and control of financial crime;
- apply appropriate accounting principles in corporate and government settings;
- perform quantitative and qualitative analyses of economic crime data and interpret the results of these analyses;
- distinguish between ethical and unethical behavior in investigating financial crimes; and
- communicate effectively about the prevention of financial crimes.

Gregory Oliver W. Coleman
Inspector General, Liberian National Police

1 Financial Crime Overview, Commonalities, and Convergence

Financial Crime Overview

The world is awash in financial crime. No person or organization, public or private, secular or religious, profit or nonprofit is immune to victimization. Perpetrators of financial crime come in many forms, often using the façade of sham or shell legal entities to conduct their criminal activity.

The immense earnings of financial criminals and their global co-conspirators are impossible to calculate but easily run into the trillions of dollars annually. Notable examples of the sources of illicit profits of financial criminals are the public and private healthcare programs that many nations provide to their citizens. The United States government, for example, claims its Medicare program suffers fraud losses of about $70 billion annually or the equivalent of $192 million *daily*. Just as with other financial crimes, the fallout goes beyond the healthcare programs themselves. Higher taxes and insurance premiums, along with increased government expenses to monitor and supervise the integrity of the programs, are some of the consequences.

Much of this fraud and thousands of other similar instances worldwide is facilitated by corruption of the participants in the programs or in the public agencies that conduct them. Lax controls and auditing, poor supervision by regulators, inadequate enforcement by investigative agencies, and inattention to recovering the assets stolen by financial criminals emboldens others and breeds more financial crime.

Government agencies and private sector victims of financial crime fare poorly in recovering the funds that are taken unlawfully from government programs and from private sector victims. While estimates are inherently difficult, statistics issued by government agencies suggest that only 2–5 percent of assets that private and public sector victims lose to financial criminals are ever recovered.

Defining Financial Crime and Its Permutations

Permutations and perpetrators of financial crime constantly evolve. At any given moment, persons in all parts of the world are conceiving of new illegal ways to take money or gain economic advantage from organizational and individual victims.

Except for crimes of passion and those committed to make an ideological statement, such as terrorism, all crimes are committed to make money or gain an economic advantage. Even crimes of pure passion sometimes have a financial element, such as in the case of a person plotting the murder of a family member to claim a life insurance policy on the victim.

Most financial crimes have four phases—when the crime is being planned, when it is committed, when the proceeds are laundered, and when the victim's losses are identified and asset recovery is needed.

This book focuses mainly on crimes that have a cash or economic advantage as their primary objective. However, the book does not deal with some profit-motivated crimes, such as drug trafficking, human trafficking, illegal gambling, nuclear trafficking, prostitution, and similar offenses. While these crimes are also motivated by the desire to make money, they do not fit into the financial crime categories that are the focus of this book.

The manual covers those crimes from the point that the perpetrators possess or control the criminal proceeds. At that point, these criminals become classic financial criminals who must engage in some of the common steps that all financial criminals take. Essential to all financial criminals is the laundering of their proceeds. Money laundering is present in all financial crimes and is a common element that all financial crimes share, irrespective of how they made their money.

What is financial crime?

A good working definition may be that it is a nonviolent action that results in the unlawful taking, moving, hiding, or disguising of money or other value by the use of guile, artifice, corruption, or deception for the benefit of the perpetrator or of another.

Financial crime is a general term that covers unlawful activities ranging from improper bookkeeping to bribery, corruption, money laundering, fraud, tax evasion, and sanctions violations. Each of these categories has subsets, offshoots, or tributaries. For example, identity theft and embezzlement are subsets of fraud. Corruption exists in both the public and private sectors. Money laundering may be practiced in many ways and may involve persons in all walks of life and private and public sector organizations. One type of financial crime often overlaps another, as is discussed below in the section dealing with the commonalities of financial crime.

Financial crimes can cross national boundaries, and the investigation and prosecution of such crimes often require authorities in a number of jurisdictions to work together to bring the alleged perpetrators before the courts.

Financial crimes, sometimes referred to as "white collar" crimes, are nonviolent criminal acts that involve the theft or misuse of money. Financial crimes are sometimes considered less important than other types of crimes because there is no violence used, but they can actually have vast impacts on personal finance and even entire financial markets. White-collar crimes are nonviolent crimes committed in commercial situations by individuals, groups, or corporations for financial gain.

Section 46 of the EFCC Act 2004 defines Economic and Financial Crimes to mean

> *the non – violent criminal and illicit activity committed with the objective of earning wealth illegally either individually or in a group or organized manner thereby violating existing legislation governing economic activities of Government*

and its administration and includes any form of fraud, narcotic drug trafficking, money laundering, embezzlement, bribery, looting, and any form of corrupt malpractices, illegal arms deal, smuggling, human trafficking and child labour, illegal oil bunkering and illegal mining, tax evasion, foreign exchange malpractice including counterfeiting currency, theft of intellectual property and piracy, open market abuse, dumping of toxic wastes and prohibited goods e.t.c.

For better understanding of nature and scope of financial crime or white-collar crime, the manual review the concept of white-collar crime and modern conceptualization as discussed below.

Scope of Financial/White-Collar Crime

Determining the extent of white-collar crime is no simple task. Two factors make it particularly difficult to accurately determine how often white-collar crimes occur. First, many white-collar crimes are not reported to formal response agencies. When individuals are victims of white-collar crimes, they may not report the victimization because of shame, concerns that reporting will be futile, or a general denial that the victimization was actually criminal. When businesses or companies are victims, they may refrain from reporting out of concern about the negative publicity that comes along with "being duped" by an employee. If victims are not willing to report their victimization, their victimization experiences will not be included in official statistics.

A second factor that makes it difficult to determine the extent of white-collar crime has to do with the conceptual ambiguity surrounding the concept. Depending on how one defines white-collar crime, one would find different estimates about the extent of white-collar crime. The federal government and other government agencies offer different definitions of white-collar crime than many scholars and researchers might use. The result is that white-collar crime researchers typically observe caution when relying on official statistics or **victimization surveys** to determine the extent of white-collar crime victimization. Despite this caution, the three main ways that we learn about the extent of white-collar crime are from official statistics provided by government agencies, victimization surveys, and research studies focusing on specific types of white-collar crime.

A word of caution is needed in reviewing these estimates. Not all criminologists agree that these offenses are appropriate indicators of white-collar crimes. Many of these offenses may have occurred outside of the scope of employment. Also because the official statistics does not capture information about offender status, it is not possible to classify the crimes according to the occupational systems where the offenses occurred.

Victimization surveys offer an opportunity to overcome some of these problems. These surveys sample residents and estimate the extent of victimization from the survey findings. While it is difficult to gauge the extent of white-collar crime, all indications are that these offenses occur with great regularity. The regularity of these offenses exacerbates their consequences.

Technology Changes the Complexion of Financial Crime

Financial crime is not static. It evolves and adapts to circumstances and opportunities. Identity theft, for example, is not a new type of crime, but the advancement of technology has spurred its growth and made it a global menace. Similarly, cybercrime did not exist before the arrival of computer technology, the Internet, and the World Wide Web.

Financial crime today is more extensive, complex, and technology-driven than ever before. So are the government and private sector efforts against it. Investigative and enforcement procedures and regulatory measures that seek to block or detect financial crime need to grow at the pace of the evolving techniques of financial criminals.

New laws and regulations, multinational agreements, treaties and conventions, and working groups are all aimed at financial crime. Nongovernmental organizations, such as the Financial Action Task Force (FATF), the Egmont Group, Interpol, and others have been formed in the past quarter-century to help public and private sector organizations to combat financial crime. Starting in 1990, with the creation of the US Financial Crimes Enforcement Network (FinCEN), nations began creating agencies that have come to be known as Financial Intelligence Units (FIUs) that facilitate international information sharing and cooperation. The success of these efforts often depends on the political will of nations to accept, adopt, and enforce them.

The patchwork of national and international requirements and standards places on financial institutions, businesses, and other organizations the duty to monitor, investigate report, train and remediate, all at a significant cost.

Even in the face of these mighty defensive and offensive efforts composed of private and public sector organizations, financial crime continues to grow. Financial criminals are industrious and find weaknesses, loopholes, negligence, or corruption to facilitate their crimes.

Globalization of Financial Crime

Financial crime flourishes when it crosses national borders. By crossing these borders, the financial criminal complicates law enforcement efforts by forcing the agencies of one country to obtain the cooperation of their counterparts in other countries for the purpose of gathering evidence or locating suspects and witnesses. When financial crime crosses national boundaries, it usually causes the pertinent authorities to seek the assistance of an international treaty, convention, or agreement, or an international organization such as Interpol.

This takes extra time, which favors the financial criminal. As time passes, the financial criminal is better able to find refuge for the financial crime proceeds, tamper with the evidence, and even seek safe haven for himself.

The more than sixty "secrecy havens" around the globe, ranging from obscure islands like Nauru and Tortola, to long-standing havens like Lichtenstein and Switzerland, are a convenient and vital resource for financial criminals that facilitate the movement and hiding of criminal assets. They provide financial criminals a crucial resource in the end-game that completes his crime.

Financial/White-Collar Crime: An Evolving Concept

While Edwin Sutherland is the pioneer of the study of financial crime or white-collar crime, the development of the field and the introduction of the concept of white-collar crime did not occur in a vacuum. Indeed, prior academic work and societal changes influenced Sutherland's scholarship, and his scholarship, in turn, has had an enormous influence on criminology and criminal justice. Tracing the source of the concept of financial crime/white-collar crime and describing its subsequent variations helps to demonstrate the importance of conceptualizing various forms of white-collar misconduct.

Sutherland was not the first social scientist to write about crimes by those in the upper class. In his 1934 *Criminology* text, Sutherland used the term "white-collar criminaloid" in reference to the "criminaloid concept" initially used by E. A. Ross (1907) in *Sin and Society*. Focusing on businessmen who engaged in harmful acts under the mask of respectability, Ross further wrote that the criminaloid is "society's most dangerous foe, more redoubtable by far than the plain criminal, because he sports the livery of virtue and operates on a titanic scale." Building on these ideas, Sutherland called attention to the fact that crimes were not committed only by members of the lower class. As noted in the introduction, Sutherland (1949) defined white-collar crime as "crime committed by a person of respectability and high social status in the course of his occupation."

Sutherland's appeal to social scientists to expand their focus to include crimes by upper-class offenders was both applauded and criticized. On the one hand, Sutherland was lauded for expanding the focus of the social sciences. On the other hand, the way that Sutherland defined and studied white-collar crime was widely criticized by a host of social scientists and legal experts. Much of the criticism centered around five concerns that scholars had about Sutherland's use of the white-collar crime concept. These concerns included (1) conceptual ambiguity, (2) empirical ambiguity, (3) methodological ambiguity, (4) legal ambiguity, and (5) policy ambiguity.

In terms of *conceptual ambiguity*, critics have noted that white-collar crime was vaguely and loosely defined by Sutherland (Robin 1974). Robin further argued that the vagueness surrounding the definition fostered ambiguous use of the term and vague interpretations by scholars and practitioners alike. Focusing on the link between scholarship and practice, one author suggested that the concept was "totally inadequate" to characterize the kinds of behavior that are at the root of the phenomena. Further describing the reactions to this conceptual ambiguity, white-collar crime scholar David Friedrichs (2002) wrote, "Perhaps no other area of criminological theory has been more plagued by conceptual confusion than that of white-collar crime."

Criticism about Sutherland's work also focused on the *empirical ambiguity* surrounding the concept. In effect, some argued that the concept only minimally reflected reality. For example, one author said that Sutherland's definition underestimated the influence of poverty on other forms of crime (Mannheim 1949). Another author argued that by focusing on the offender (in terms of status) and the location (the workplace) rather than the offense, the concept did not accurately reflect the behaviors that needed to be addressed (Edelhertz 1983). Edelhertz went as far as to suggest that this vague empirical conceptualization created barriers with practitioners and resulted in a lack of research on white-collar crime between the 1950s and 1970s. Shapiro (1990) also recognized the problems that the conceptualization of white-collar crime created for future researchers. She wrote:

> *The concept has done its own cognitive mischief.*
> *It… is founded on a spurious correlation that causes*
> *sociologists to misunderstand the structural impetus*
> *for these offenses, the problems the offenses create for*

> *systems of social control, and the sources and con-*
> *sequences of class bias in the legal system. (p. 346)*

The consequences of this empirical ambiguity are such that findings from white-collar crime studies sometimes call into question the nature of white-collar offenders. One study of white-collar offenders convicted in seven federal districts between 1976 and 1978, for example, found that most offenses described as white-collar were actually "committed by those who fall in the middle classes of our society."

Sutherland was also criticized for *methodological ambiguity*. He defined white-collar crime as behaviors committed by members of the upper class, but his research focused on all sorts of offenses including workplace theft, fraud by mechanics, deception by shoe sales persons, and crimes by corporations. One might say that Sutherland committed a "bait and switch" in defining one type of crime but actually researching another variety.

A fourth criticism of Sutherland's white-collar crime scholarship can be termed *legal ambiguity*. Some legal scholars contended that the concept was too sociological at the expense of legal definitions of white-collar offending. To some, white-collar crimes should be narrowly defined to include those behaviors that are criminally illegal. Some even take it a step farther and suggest that white-collar criminals are those individuals convicted of white-collar crimes (suggesting that if one were not caught for a white-collar crime one actually committed, then one would not be a white-collar criminal). Sutherland, and others, have countered this argument by suggesting that conviction is irrelevant in determining whether behaviors constitute white-collar crimes.

A final criticism of the white-collar crime concept is related to the *policy ambiguity* surrounding the concept. In particular, some have argued that the vagueness of the definition and its purely academic focus created a disconnect between those developing policies and practices responding to white-collar crime and those studying white-collar crime. Over the past decade or so, criminologists have become more vocal about the need for evidence-based practices to guide criminal justice policies and activities. In terms of white-collar crime, an issue that has been cited is that unclear definitions about white-collar crime make it extremely difficult for policy makers and practitioners to use criminological information to guide policy development and criminal justice practices. In effect, how can criminologists call for evidence-based practices for certain types of crime when they have not adequately provided the evidence needed to develop subsequent practices?

Sutherland was aware of the concerns about the concept potentially being vague. He noted that his point was not precision but to note how white-collar crime is "identical in its general characteristics with other crime rather than different from it" (Sutherland 1941, p. 112). He wrote:

> *The purpose of the concept of white-collar crime is to call attention to a vast area of criminal behavior which is generally overlooked as criminal behavior, which is seldom brought within the score of the theories of criminal behavior, and which, when included, call for modifications in the usual theories of criminal behavior.*

Thus, Sutherland conceded that the concept was vague in nature, but it was necessarily vague in order to promote further discussion about the concept. Sutherland was successful in promoting further discussion about the phenomena, though the topic received very little attention in the 1950s and 1960s. This began to change in the early 1970s when criminologists Marshall Clinard and Richard Quinney published *Criminal Behavior Systems*. Building on Sutherland's work, Clinard and Quinney (1973) argued that white-collar crime can be divided into two types: corporate crime and occupational crime. They focused their definition of *corporate crime* on illegal behaviors that are committed by employees of a corporation to benefit the corporation, company, or business. In contrast, they defined *occupational crime* as "violations of legal codes in the course of activity in a legitimate occupation." By distinguishing between crimes by corporations and crimes against corporations, Clinard and Quinney took an important step in addressing some of the ambiguity surrounding the white-collar crime concept. Indeed, corporate crime and occupational crime are viewed as "the two principal or 'pure' forms of white-collar crime."

After Clinard and Quinney's work, white-collar crime research by criminologists escalated in the 1970s and 1980s. Much of this research focused on ways to conceptualize and define the phenomenon in ways that addressed the criticisms surrounding Sutherland's definition. Table 1.1 shows eight different concepts and definitions that criminologists have used to describe these behaviors. Just as Sutherland's definition was criticized, each of the concepts provided in Table 1.1 are imperfect. Still, they illustrate the impact that Sutherland's white-collar crime scholarship has had on criminology and criminal justice.

This is troublesome for at least five reasons. First, the lack of a sound definition of white-collar crime has hindered detection efforts. Second, without a concrete definition of white-collar crime, the most effective responses to the problem cannot be gauged.

Third, varying definitions among researchers have made it difficult to draw comparisons between different white-collar crime studies. Fourth, vague conceptualizations have made it more difficult to identify the causes of the behavior. Finally, varied definitions of white-collar crime have made it difficult to determine with accuracy the true extent of white-collar crime.

Modern Conceptualizations of White-Collar Crime

Today, criminologists and social scientists offer various ways to define white-collar crime (see Figure 1.1). These variations tend to overlap with one another and include the following:

- White-collar crime as moral or ethical violations
- White-collar crime as social harm
- White-collar crime as violations of criminal law
- White-collar crime as violations of civil law
- White-collar crime as violations of regulatory laws
- White-collar crime as workplace deviance
- White-collar crime as definitions socially constructed by businesses
- White-collar crime as research definitions
- White-collar crime as official government definitions
- White-collar crime as violations of trust
- White-collar crime as occupational crimes
- White-collar crime as violations occurring in occupational systems

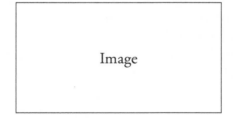

Defining *white-collar crime as moral or ethical violations* follows ideals inherent within principles of what is known as natural law. *Natural law* focuses on behaviors or activities that are defined as wrong because they violate the ethical principles of a particular culture, subculture, or group. The immoral nature of the activities is seen as the foundation for defining certain types of white-collar activities as criminal. Some individuals, for example, define any business activities that destroy animal life or plant life as immoral and unethical.

To those individuals, the behaviors of individuals and businesses participating in those activities would be defined as white-collar crimes.

Some prefer to define *white-collar crime as violations of criminal law*. From this framework, white-collar crimes are criminally illegal behaviors committed by upper class individuals during the course of their occupation. From a systems perspective, those working in the criminal justice system would likely define white-collar crime as criminally illegal behaviors. Crime, in this context, is defined as "an intentional act or omission committed in violation of the criminal law without defense or justification and sanctioned by the state as a felony or misdemeanour." Applying a criminal law definition to white-collar crime, white-collar crimes are those criminally illegal acts committed during the course of one's job. Here are a few examples:

- An accountant embezzles funds from his employer.
- Two nurses steal drugs from their workplace and sell them to addicts.
- A financial investor steals investors' money.
- A prosecutor accepts a bribe to drop criminal charges.
- Two investors share inside information that allow them to redirect their stock purchases.
- A disgruntled employee destroys the computer records of a firm upon her resignation.

These acts are instances where the criminal law has been violated during the course of employment. As such, members of the criminal justice could be called upon to address those misdeeds.

Certainly, some rule breaking during the course of employment does not rise to the level of criminal behavior, but it may violate civil laws. Consequently, some may define *white-collar crime as violations of civil law*. Consider cases of corporate wrongdoing against consumers. In those situations, it is rare that the criminal law would be used to respond to the offending corporation. More often, cases are brought into the civil justice system.

Individuals have also defined *white-collar crime as violations of regulatory law*. Some workplace misdeeds might not violate criminal or civil laws but may violate a particular occupation's regulatory laws. Most occupations and businesses have standards, procedures, and regulations that are designed to administratively guide and direct workplace activities. The nursing home industry provides a good example. The government has developed a set of standards that nursing home administrators are expected to follow in providing care to nursing home residents. At different times during the year, government officials inspect nursing homes to see if they are abiding by the regulations. In most instances, some form of wrongdoing is uncovered. These instances of wrongdoing, however, are not violations of criminal law or civil law; rather, they are violations of regulatory law. Hence, some authors focus on white-collar crimes as violations of regulatory laws.

Sometimes behaviors performed as part of an occupational routine might be wrong but not necessarily illegal by criminal, civil, or regulatory definitions. As a result, some prefer to follow definitions of *white-collar crime as workplace deviance.* This is a broader way to define white-collar crime, and such an approach would include all of those workplace acts that violate the norms or standards of the workplace, regardless of whether they are formally defined as illegal or not. Violations of criminal, civil, and regulatory laws would be included, as would those violations that are set by the workplace itself. Beyond those formal violations of the law, consider the following situations as examples of workplace deviance:

- A professor cancels a class simply because he doesn't feel like going to class.
- A worker takes a thirty-minute break when she was only supposed to take a fifteen-minute break.
- A worker calls his boss and says he is too sick to come to work when in fact he is not actually sick (but he uses that "fake sick voice" as part of his ploy).
- A wedding photographer gets drunk at a client's wedding, takes horrible pictures, and hits on the groom.
- An author uses silly examples to try to get his point across.

In each of these cases, no laws have necessarily been broken; however, one could argue that workplace or occupational norms may have been violated.

Somewhat related, one can also define *white-collar crime as definitions socially constructed by businesses*. What this means is that a particular company or business might define behaviors that it believes to be improper. What is wrong in one company might not necessarily be wrong in another company. Some businesses might have formal dress codes while others might have casual Fridays. Some companies might tolerate workers taking small quantities of the goods it produces home each night, while other companies might define that behavior as inappropriate and criminal. The expectations for workplace behavior, then, are defined by the workplace. Incidentally, some experts have suggested that expectations be defined in such a way as to accept at least minor forms of wrongdoing. The basis for this suggestion is that individuals are more satisfied with their jobs if they are able to break the rules of their job at least every now and then. As a simple example, where would you rather work (1) in a workplace that lets you get away with longer breaks every now and then or (2) in a workplace where you are docked double pay for every minute you take over the allotted break?

In some cases, workplace behaviors might not be illegal or deviant but might actually create forms of harm for various individuals. As a result, some prefer to define *white-collar crime as social harm*. Those defining white-collar crime from this perspective are more concerned with the harm done by occupational activities than whether behavior is defined either formally or informally as illegal or deviant. Additional examples of white-collar crimes that are examples of this social harm perspective are the following "crimes" that occur without law-breaking occurring—cross-border malpractices, asymmetrical environmental regulations, corrupt practices, child labor in impoverished communities, and pharmaceutical practices such as those allowing testing of drugs in third-world countries.

Another way to define these behaviors is to consider *white-collar crime as research definitions*. When researchers study and gather data about white-collar crime, they must operationalize or define white-collar crime in a way that allows them to reliably and validly measure the behavior. The researchers defined white-collar crime as "illegal or unethical acts that violate fiduciary responsibility or public trust for personal or organizational gain" (Kane & Wall 2006). Using this definition as their foundation, the researchers were able to conduct a study that measured the characteristics of white-collar crime, its consequences, and contributing factors. Note that had they chosen a different definition, their results may have been different. The way that we define phenomena will influence the observations we make about those phenomena.

Another way to define these behaviors is to consider *white-collar crime as official government definitions.* Government agencies and employees of those agencies will have definitions of white-collar crime that may or may not parallel the way others define white-collar crime. The Federal Bureau of Investigation (FBI), for example, has used an offense-based perspective to define white-collar crime as part of its Uniform Crime Reporting program. The FBI defines white-collar crime as

> *Those illegal acts which are characterized by deceit, concealment, or violation of trust and which are not dependent upon the application or threat of physical force or violence. Individuals and organizations commit these acts to obtain money, property, or services; to avoid payment or loss of money or services; or to secure personal or business advantage. (United States Department of Justice, 1989, p. 3; as cited in Barnett, no date)*

In following this definition, the FBI tends to take a broader definition of white-collar crime than many white-collar crime scholars and researchers do. Identity theft offers a case in point. The FBI includes identity theft as a white-collar crime type. Some academics, however, believe that such a classification is inappropriate. One research team conducted interviews with fifty-nine convicted identity thieves and found that offenses and offenders did not meet the traditional characteristics of white-collar crimes or white-collar offenders. Many offenders were unemployed and working independently, meaning their offenses were not committed as part of a legitimate occupation, or in the course of their occupation.

Another way to define white-collar crime is to focus on *white-collar crime as violations of trust* that occur during the course of legitimate employment. Criminologist Susan Shapiro (1990) has argued for the need to view white-collar crime as abuses of trust, and she suggests that researchers should focus on the *act* rather than the *actor*. She wrote:

> *Offenders clothed in very different wardrobes lie, steal, falsify, fabricate, exaggerate, omit, deceive, dissemble, shirk, embezzle, misappropriate, self-deal, and engage in corruption or incompliance by misusing their positions of trust. It turns out most of them are not upper class. (p. 358)*

In effect, Shapiro was calling for a broader definition of white-collar crime that was not limited to the collar of the offender's shirts.

Others have also called for broader conceptualizations that are not limited to wardrobes or occupational statuses. Following Clinard and Quinney's 1973 conceptualization, some have suggested that these behaviors be classified as *white-collar crimes as occupational crimes.* One author defines occupational crimes as "violations that occur during the course of occupational activity and are related to employment" (Robin 1974). Robin argued vehemently for the broader conceptualization of white-collar crime. He noted that various forms of lower-class workplace offenses "are more similar to white-collar crime methodologically than behaviorally," suggesting that many occupational offenders tend to use the same methods to commit their transgressions. He further stated that the failure of scholars to broadly conceive white-collar crime "results in underestimating the amount of crime, distorts relative frequencies of the typology of crimes, produces a biased profile of the personal and social characteristics of the violators, and thus affects our theory of criminality."

Criminologist Gary Green (1990) has been a strong advocate of focusing on occupational crime rather than a limited conceptualization of white-collar crime. He defined occupational crime as "any act punishable by law which is committed through opportunity created in the course of an occupation that is legal" (p. 13). Green described four varieties of occupational crime: (1) organizational occupational crimes, which include crimes by corporations; (2) state authority occupational crimes, which include crimes by governments; (3) professional occupational crimes, which include those crimes by individuals in upper class jobs; and (4) individual occupational crimes, which include those crimes committed by individuals in lower class jobs. The strength of his conceptualization is that it expands white-collar crime to consider all forms of misdeeds committed by employees and businesses during the course of employment.

Using each of the above definitions as a framework, white-collar crime can also be defined as *violations occurring in occupational systems*. This text uses such a framework to provide broad systems perspective about white-collar crime. White-collar crime can therefore be defined as "any violation of criminal, civil, or regulatory laws—or deviant, harmful, or unethical actions—committed during the course of employment in various occupational systems." This definition allows us to consider numerous types of workplace misconduct and the interactions between these behaviors and broader systems involved in preventing and responding to white-collar crimes. As will be shown in the following paragraphs, the extent of these crimes is enormous.

Commonalities of All Financial Crimes

There are many types of financial crime, such as money laundering, fraud, and corruption, each with distinct subsets, such as terrorism and threat finance, identity theft, and commercial bribery. But they all share several constant commonalities. These commonalities make them more alike than dissimilar.

Recognizing and exploiting the commonalities helps private and public sector organizations build a cohesive, comprehensive, and collaborative approach to financial crime and maybe better results. The issue of convergence is discussed below in this lecture.

Financial crimes have these commonalities:

All financial crimes involve money laundering. At some point in the planning and execution of financial crimes, all of them involve money laundering. A business involved in a foreign corrupt payment, a public official who receives illicit payments, a violator of sanctions laws, an identity thief, and other financial criminals, at some point, must hide or disguise the criminal proceeds or the domestic or international movement of "clean" money for the purpose of committing a financial crime. Money laundering is a necessary function of the financial criminal because it permits him to mask his involvement in the financial crime, evade the payment of taxes, and move the money to hide it from victims and the government authorities. The broad reach of most money laundering laws and the predicate crimes that activate prosecutions for money laundering, as well as the international money laundering control standards of the Financial Action Task Force (FATF) and other world bodies, lend credibility to the fact that all financial crimes involve money laundering.

All financial crimes result in tax evasion. It would be a unique financial criminal who would go to great lengths of stealing and disguising his gains and still declare his criminal proceeds in an income tax return. The evasion of taxes is committed by the parties on both sides of most financial crime transactions, such as those involving corruption. Where a transaction involves official corruption, for example, tax evasion is usually committed by both parties of the transaction. The corrupter falsifies its tax return by mischaracterizing the withdrawal or transmission of funds or the generation of cash destined for the corrupt official. The public official who receives the corrupt payment will either not report the income or falsify its source on the tax returns that he may file.

Tax evasion is not only a financial crime in its own right, but it is also a by-product of other crimes. The Financial Action Task Force announced in February 2012 that it was expanding its "40 Recommendations" on money laundering after twenty-two years to include recommendation for measures against tax evasion. This can be viewed as an important validation that financial crime and tax evasion are intertwined.

Apart from this important step toward a more active world effort against tax evasion, the enactment of far-reaching tax compliance laws with a multinational reach, like the landmark US Foreign Account Tax Compliance Act (FATCA) of 2010, is a harbinger of a more active multinational assault on tax evasion and its arrival as a top international priority. These landmark developments, symbolized by FATCA, which touches financial institutions worldwide, are among the major financial crime developments of the early part of the twenty-first century.

All financial crimes require a financial institution. No financial crime of any magnitude can be carried out without a financial institution. The term "financial institution" covers more than banks. In the broad sense, it also includes private banks, credit unions, cooperative institutions, securities dealers, insurance companies, commodities traders, money transmitters, and other entities where the public can conduct financial transactions.

The Financial Action Task Force resources offer a wealth of information on financial crime, including the wide range of financial institutions that financial criminals use. The FATF also publishes a wide range of financial crime typologies and commentaries that financial crime specialists will find helpful. The many types of financial institutions and businesses that are implicated in financial crime cases attest to the indispensability of financial institutions to financial criminals and the diversity of them.

The vulnerability of these businesses to be leveraged in a financial crime is compounded by the risks that their employees, who may be corrupted or compromised, present. All institutions and businesses face this common threat of the "enemy within." These are the employees or insiders that can compromise operations, steal, or leak confidential information, corrupt internal processes, rig technological settings and programs, weaken organizational defences, assist inside or outside financial criminals, and inflict harm that their unique position enables them to carry out.

A corrupt or compromised employee can wreck as much havoc or more in a private or public sector organization as any outside financial criminal can. The irony is that despite this ability to inflict so much harm, employees or insiders often receive far less screening and due diligence examination than customers before they are placed on the job. Financial institutions spend significant time and money on due diligence reviews focused on customers, but for employees or other insiders, they spend relatively little in pre-employment screening and post-employment monitoring. Employees are often hired with the prior review and approval of only human resources departments. Investigation and vigilance of post-employment employee and insider conduct is usually the responsibility of corporate security departments.

Financial criminals appreciate the value of a complicit insider and are eager to promote the employment of an accomplice by an organization that they are targeting.

All financial crimes interface with government agencies. Every financial crime produces or activates a preexisting interface for a financial institution or affected business with a government agency. For most financial institutions, a regulatory or supervisory agency that oversees compliance will normally need to be informed of the occurrence of the financial crime or of the suspicion of a financial crime in a Suspicious Activity Report1 (SAR) or other communication with an agency.

If a financial crime occurs at or through a business that is not required to file suspicious activity reports, the business will invariably interface with a government agency when agents arrive to investigate the crime or seek records pertaining to the crime.

In most countries, data from suspicious activity reports and other government reporting forms are processed through government "financial intelligence units." More than 120 nations have FIUs, which band together in a confederation known as the Egmont Group2. The Group facilitates the exchange of data and intelligence among its members, under security protocols, with the goal of improving multinational efforts against financial crime.

All financial crimes create the need for asset recovery. All financial crime leaves someone poorer than they were before. The major recent financial crimes, such as the Bernard Madoff Ponzi scheme, the international bank mega-fraud of Allen Stanford, the legal settlements scheme of Scott Rothstein, and others have left behind tens of thousands of victims with billions of dollars in losses.

Thousands of less-celebrated financial criminals worldwide leave millions of other victims behind. Victims that have the resources to attempt to recover their assets rarely succeed in these efforts. Government agencies that seek to recover funds that are stolen from government programs are no more successful in their efforts despite the strong asset recovery and legal and judicial weapons they possess.

Asset recovery is the neglected art of the financial crime continuum. The failure to recover the assets taken by financial criminals is a primary cause of the growth of financial crime. The deterrent effect that successful asset recovery could achieve is missing. Financial criminals have the pleasant reality that they rarely are required to relinquish the money they take from their victims— even if they go to prison.

These are known as Suspicious Transaction Reports (STRs) in many jurisdictions. To learn more, please click here: www.egmont-group.org.

All (major) financial crimes involve more than one country. Whether it is the location of the financial crime victim or the base of operations of the financial criminal or his co-conspirators or the home of the financial institutions they use or the countries where the criminal proceeds moved through or were applied, all major financial crimes involve multiple countries, especially in today's electronic world.

The many bilateral agreements and multinational treaties, mutual legal assistance treaties, tax information exchange agreements, financial information exchange agreements, intergovernmental agreements, extradition treaties, and other international cooperative agreements that bear on financial crime underscore the international nature of these crimes.

Some laws have an international focus by definition or by their very name. The US Foreign Corrupt Practices Act (FCPA) is an example. The placement of law enforcement agents of a country in their nation's embassies overseas and the work of international organizations, such as Interpol and the FATF, all highlight the cross-border nature of major financial crimes.

Financial crime often involves public or private sector corruption. Nothing facilitates financial crime more than a corrupt or complicit business insider or public official. Corruption is the engine that drives most major international financial crime. Appreciation of the corrosive effect of corruption has moved many organizations to mount a broad, still blossoming assault on corruption in recent years, as evidenced in part by the revised 40 Recommendations of the Financial Action Task Force. Global anti-corruption is covered in its own chapter of the manual.

Public and private–sector corruption has many variations. Examples include the unlawful payment by a business to the employee of another business to obtain trade secrets or the bribery of a regulator to turn a blind eye to criminal activity in a financial institution or other type of business.

Capitalizing On the "Commonalities" and Exploring "Convergence"

By examining these commonalities, financial crime specialists in the distinct component fields of anti–money laundering (AML), fraud, global anti-corruption, and others can determine if adoption of a coordinated, integrated approach and away from a splintered or siloed approach that now characterizes financial crime efforts is advisable. Currently, the detection, prevention, regulatory, and enforcement efforts directed at financial crime follows the siloed approach. A unified or "converged" approach may allow private and public entities to end underutilization of disciplines and allow internal units to achieve greater efficiency, economies, and effectiveness.

Understanding and appreciating the commonalities can lead to development of a cohesive, more effective global approach to financial crime in public and private sector entities. The culmination of this approach comes in the creation of converged units with titles like the Financial Crime Risk Management Group within institutions and organizations. This approach has the potential to improve results, streamline procedures, upgrade utility of information and intelligence, increase collaboration among diverse employees and organizations, and save money.

The unification of functions that now operate separately could allow fraud investigators to learn and capitalize on monitoring tools used by AML analysts and at the same time provide the AML analysts and others access to the investigative expertise of persons in the fraud units.

If the common bonds that financial crimes share make the case for a centralized approach, then convergence may be the best course of action. The commonalities seem to justify a deep examination of the way financial crimes are dealt with by private and public sector entities. They call for a streamlined, unified effort that improves effectiveness.

Consequences of White-Collar Crime

Crime, by its very nature, has consequences for individuals and communities. Financial/white-collar crime, in particular, has a set of consequences that may be significantly different from the kinds of consequences that arise from street crimes. In particular, the consequences can be characterized as (1) individual economic losses, (2) societal economic losses, (3) emotional consequences, (4) physical harm, and (5) "positive" consequences.

Individual economic losses refer to the losses that individual victims or business lose due to white-collar crimes. One way that criminologists have captured these losses is to compare them to losses experienced by victims of conventional crimes. By some estimates, the average amount lost to embezzlement, for example, is about $1,000,000 ("The Marquette Report," 2009). By comparison, consider the following:

- The average street/highway robbery entails losses of $1,032.
- The average gas station robbery entails losses of $1,007.

- The average convenience store robbery entails losses of $712 (Federal Bureau of Investigation, 2009b).

It is important to note that a small group of offenders can create large dollar losses. In fact, Sutherland (1949) argued that white-collar crimes cost several times more than street crimes in terms of financial losses. While his estimate may be a little dated, the fact remains that a white-collar crime will likely cause larger dollar losses to victims than a street crime would.

Societal economic losses entail the total amount of losses incurred by society from white-collar crime. In terms of business failures, one estimate suggests that one-third to one-half of business failures are attributed to employee theft (National White Collar Crime Center, 2009). With regard to recovery costs, taxpayers pay billions of dollars to support the efforts of the criminal, civil, and regulatory justice systems. As an illustration of how these costs can quickly add up, one white-collar criminal involved in a $7 million Ponzi scheme eventually lost everything and was unable to afford his own attorney. In this case, the federal public defender's office was assigned the task of representing the accused. Attorney costs in white-collar crime cases are believed to be particularly exorbitant.

Emotional consequences are also experienced by victims of white-collar crime and all members of society exposed to this misconduct. These emotional consequences include stress from victimization, violation of trust, and damage to public morale. With regard to stress, any experience of victimization is stressful, but the experience of white-collar crime victimization is believed to be particularly stressful. Much of the stress stems from the violation of trust that comes along with white-collar crimes.

According to Sutherland (1941), the violation of trust can be defined as the "most general" characteristic of white-collar crime. Victims of a street robbery didn't trust the stranger who robbed them in the first place. Victims of a white-collar crime, in addition to the other losses incurred from the victimization, have their trust violated by the offender. There is reason to believe that the level of trust may be tied to the specific level of trust given to different types of white-collar offenders (e.g., we trust doctors and pharmacists at a certain level but auto mechanics on another level). Building on Sutherland's ideas, Moore and Mills (1990) described the following consequences of white-collar crime:

- Diminished faith in a free economy and in business leaders
- Erosion of public morality
- Loss of confidence in political institutions, processes, and leaders

Physical harm may also result from white-collar crime victimization. Sometimes, physical harm may be a direct result of the white-collar offense. For example, cases of physical or sexual patient abuse will result in physical harm for victims. Other times, experiencing financial harm can lead to physical problems. The loss of one's entire retirement savings, for example, has been found to contribute to health problems for white-collar crime victims. Death or serious physical injury is also a possible consequence of white-collar crimes.

Community integration is a fourth function of white-collar crime. In particular, groups of individuals who otherwise would not have become acquainted with one another may come together in their response to white-collar crime. When there is a crime outbreak in a neighborhood, those neighbors come together to share their experiences and make their neighborhood stronger. A crime outbreak in a business could have the same result. Coworkers who never talked with one another might suddenly become lunch buddies simply because they want to get together to talk about the crimes that occurred in their workplace. As well, at the societal level, new groups have been formed to prevent and respond to white-collar crime.

Conclusion

The global financial crime field is complex and rapidly evolving, but recognizing the commonalities and intersections between all financial crimes is a necessary starting point. Approaching financial crime more holistically may offer a more coordinated, efficient response in the compliance, investigative, and enforcement fields. It also serves as a means to introduce the wide range of topics that will be covered in subsequent lectures.

Take-Home Practice Menu

1. Which of the following is TRUE or FALSE concerning the financial crimes commonalities?

All financial crimes involve money laundering ❑ True ❑ False

All financial crimes result in tax avoidance ❑ True ❑ False

All financial crimes interface with-
    out government agencies ❑ True ❑ False

All financial crimes create the
    need for asset recovery ❑ True ❑ False

All (major) financial crimes involve
    more than one country ❑ True ❑ False

2. In the following statement tick TRUE or FALSE as applicable.

Permutations and perpetrators of financial crime constantly evolve [❑ True ❑ False] because financial crime is static [❑ True ❑ False]; therefore, forensic investigation professional must be ahead of the fraudsters in term of knowledge, skill, and abilities [❑ True ❑ False].

3. Which of the following is not a consequence of financial crime?
    a. Emotional consequence
    b. Physical harm
    c. Societal economic losses
    d. Individual economic law
    e. Community integration

4. Most financial crimes have four phases [❑ True ❑ False]. Identify the odd phrase.
    a. when the crime is being planned

b. when it is committed
c. when to commit the crime
d. when the proceeds are laundered
e. when the victim's losses are identified and asset recovery is needed

5. Determining the extent of financial crime is no simple task. Two factors make it particularly difficult to accurately determine how often white-collar crimes occur.
Identify the two factors from the following
   a. Financial crimes are not reported to formal response agencies; and difficulty in determining the extent of financial crimes has to do with the conceptual ambiguity surrounding the concept.
   b. Financial crimes are not reported to formal response agencies; and non-available official statistics record from government agencies.
   c. Difficulty in determining the extent of financial crimes has to do with the conceptual ambiguity surrounding the concept; and non-available official statistics record from government agencies.
   d. Difficulty in determining the extent of financial crimes has to do with the conceptual ambiguity surrounding the concept; and non-available official statistics record from government agencies.
   e. Non-available official statistics record and victimization surveys from government agencies.

6. Three main ways that we learn about the extent of financial crimes are EXCEPT
   a. official statistics provided by government agencies
   b. victimization surveys
   c. estimates
   d. research studies focusing on specific types of financial crimes

7. Criminologists and social scientists offer various ways to define white-collar crimes.

   These variations tend to overlap with one another and include the following EXCEPT

   a. White-collar crime as moral or ethical violations
   b. White-collar crime as society menace
   c. White-collar crime as definitions socially constructed by businesses
   d. White-collar crime as occupational crimes
   e. White-collar crime as violations occurring in occupational systems

(For the answers, please turn to Appendix A)

2 Types of Financial Crimes

Introduction

There are many types of financial crimes. Some of these crimes can be solved in a short period, while others will take a long time. The time required directly relates to the complexity of the crime. Complex financial crimes consume large amounts of time to gather huge amounts of financial records to support a conviction. However, all financial crimes have one common factor: greed. Most people are honest and trustworthy when the opportunity is not present.

There are three factors that are present in financial crimes: (1) something of value must be present; (2) an opportunity to take something of value without being detected must be present; and (3) there must be a perpetrator who is willing to commit the offense. Financial crimes or white-collar crimes include but are not limited to the following four main categories:

- Corruption—the giving, requesting, receiving, or accepting of an improper advantage related to a position or office, e.g., kickbacks, bribery, organizational, or public corruption.
- Fraud—an intentional perversion of truth for the purpose of inducing another in reliance upon it to part with some valuable thing belonging to him or to surrender a legal right, e.g., bank fraud, consumer fraud, credit card fraud.
- Theft—the illegal taking of another person's property without the victim's consent, e.g., cash theft, inventory theft.

- Manipulation—a means of gaining illegal control or influence over others' activities, means, and results, e.g., bankruptcy crime, bid rigging, competition crime, computer crime, counterfeit currency, cybercrime, ghost employees, inflated invoices, and income tax crime.

These four main categories of financial crimes are briefly explained below.

Fraud Crime

Fraud can be defined as an intentional perversion of truth for the purpose of inducing another in reliance upon it to part with some valuable thing belonging to him or to surrender a legal right. Fraud is unlawful and intentional making of a misrepresentation, which causes actual prejudice or which is potentially prejudicial to another.

Advance Fee Fraud

Victims are approached by letter, faxes, or e-mail without prior contact. Victims' addresses are obtained from telephone and e-mail directories, business journals, magazines, and newspapers. A typical advance fraud letter describes the need to move funds out of Nigeria or some other sub-Saharan African country, usually the recovery of contractual funds, crude oil shipments, or inheritance from late kings or governors. This is an external kind of fraud, where advance fee fraudsters attempt to secure a prepaid commission for an arrangement that is never actually fulfilled or work that is never done.

Victims are often naïve and greedy, or, at worst, prepared to abet serious criminal offences such as looting public money from a poor African state. The advance fee fraud has been around for centuries, most famously in the form of the Spanish prisoner scam (Ampratwum 2009, 68):

> *In this, a wealthy merchant would be contacted by a stranger who was seeking help in smuggling a fictitious family member out of a Spanish jail. In exchange for funding the 'rescue' the merchant was promised a reward, which of course, never materialized.*

Advance fee fraud is expanding quickly on the Internet. The advent of the Internet and proliferation of its use in the last decades makes it an attractive medium for communicating the fraud, enabling a worldwide reach. Advance fee fraudsters tend to employ specific methods that exploit the bounded rationality and automatic behaviour of victims. Methods include assertion of authority and expert power, referencing respected persons and organizations, providing partial proof of legitimacy, creating urgency, and implying scarcity and privilege.

Bank Fraud

Bank fraud is a criminal offence of knowingly executing a scheme to defraud a financial institution. For example in China, bank fraud is expected to increase both in complexity and in quantity as criminals keep upgrading their fraud methods and techniques. Owing to the strong penal emphasis of Chinese criminal law, harsh punishment including death penalty and life imprisonment has been used frequently for serious bank fraud and corruption. The uncertain law and inconsistent enforcement practices have made offenders more fatalistic about the matter, simply hoping they will not be the unlucky ones to get caught.

Financial fraud in the banking sector is criminal acts often linked to financial instruments in that investors are deceived into investing money in a financial instrument that is said to yield a high profit. Investors lose their money because no investment actually takes place; the instrument does not exist; the investment cannot produce the promised profit; or it is a very high-risk investment unknown to the investor. The money is usually divided between the person who talked the investor into the deal and the various middlemen, who all played a part in the scheme.

Cheque Fraud

When a company cheque is stolen, altered, or forged, it may be diverted to an unauthorized person who accesses the funds and then closes the account or simply disappears.

Click Fraud

This occurs when an individual or computer program fraudulently clicks on an online advertisement without any intention of learning more about the advertiser or making a purchase. When you click on an advertisement displayed by a search engine, the advertiser typically pays a fee for each click, which is supposed to direct potential buyers to its product. Click fraud has become a serious problem at Google and other websites that feature pay-per-click online advertising. Some companies hire third parties (typically from low-wage countries) to fraudulently click on a competitor's advertisements to weaken them by driving up their marketing costs. Click fraud can also be perpetrated with software programs doing the clicking.

Consumer Fraud

These are attempts to coerce consumers into paying for goods not received or goods that are substandard, not as specified, or at inflated prices or fees. The growing use of Internet websites, as an alternative to unsolicited phone calls or visits to potential customers, compounds this problem.

Consumer fraud is a term also used in the opposite meaning, where the consumer is fraudulent. An example is consumer insurance fraud, which is defined as a deliberate deception perpetrated against an insurance company for the purpose of financial gain. Common frauds include misrepresentation of facts on an insurance application, submission of claims for injuries or damages that never occurred, and arrangement of accidents and inflation of actual claims. Insurance fraud is a global economic problem that threatens the financial strength of insurers and threatens the survival of the insurance institutions.

Credit Card Fraud

Credit card fraud refers to the unauthorized use of a credit card to make purchases. Most stolen credit cards are stolen before they reach the intended customer, although many credit card numbers are stolen by store cashiers or other store employees.

Credit card fraud is a multimillion-dollar business that hurts businesses and the public. Most credit card fraud is controlled by organized crime. The scheme is a classic pattern. Credit cards are stolen, fenced, and sent elsewhere. Generally, the credit cards are stolen before the credit card holder is able to report its disappearance or before the issuing company is able to warn its subscribers of the theft so that they can refuse to honor them.

Credit cards are often obtained in the following ways:

- Credit card is stolen in the delivery process.
- Credit cards are stolen in the printing process or duplicated.
- Credit cards are stolen when returned to the issuer when they are refused or were undeliverable.
- Credit cards are sometimes stolen on the street like cash or checks.
- Business employees deliberately "forget" to return credit cards to their customers.
- Credit cards are counterfeited.
- Credit card numbers are copied from legitimate customers and used to make purchases.

In some cases, credit cards are counterfeited, sometimes using legitimate numbers. Stolen credit cards are used to purchase merchandise that is fenced to an illegitimate vendor. The vendor in turn sells the merchandise for cash. The cardholder is not liable for the purchases if he reports the theft to the credit card company within thirty days. One organized crime group ships the goods overseas for resale. Credit card companies report that they lose multiple millions of dollars through credit card fraud.

Embezzlement

Embezzlement occurs when one who has been entrusted with funds steals them. Embezzlement occurs when a person entrusted with funds for safekeeping, such as an estate trustee or financial manager, uses the funds without authorization for his own benefit. Embezzlement can often occur between trusted friends or even relatives but also occurs on a simple business front as well. Scrupulous examination of financial records by the estate or fund owner can help reveal signs of embezzlement, such as missing funds, duplicated checks, or accounting errors.

Hedge Fund Fraud

Hedge fund fraud may cause substantial losses for hedge fund investors. Hedge fund is defined by Muhtaseb and Yang (2008) as a pooled investment that is privately organized and administered by a professional management firm and not widely available to the public. The fund managers often invest a considerable amount of their own wealth in the funds they manage. They tend to refuse to discuss their trading strategies because they do not want competitors to imitate their moves. Muhtaseb and Yang (2008) presented the following hedge fund fraud case.

> *Samuel Israel, James Marquez and Daniel Marino set up and managed Bayou Funds in 1996. Marquez had a good reputation and was*

well connected in the industry, as he had been a former trader for the billionaire hedge fund manager George Soros. Customers invested more than $450 million in Bayou from 1996 to 2005. The leftover funds were approximately $100 million. To hide and perpetuate their fraudulent scheme, the managers knowingly misrepresented the value and performance of Bayou Funds, and issued false and misleading financial documents to investors. In 2005, Israel sent a letter to the investors that Bayou Funds would shut down at the end of the month. He said that he wanted to spend more time with his children after his divorce. Investors started asking for their money back. Israel sent another letter to explain that the process had been slowed down by auditing work because they had to make sure that the funds closed with accurate book records. The letter also stated that investors would get 90 per cent of their money back in the following week and the rest of capital a little later. However, none of the investors ever received a single penny back. The truth was revealed by Marino's suicide note typed on six pages in late 2005.

Identity Fraud

There are many reported cases where people have had to defend themselves against claims because others have stolen their identity using personal data such as social security number, address, and date of birth. Identity fraud is based on identity theft that is a crime in which an imposer obtains key pieces of personal information, such as social security identification numbers, driver's licence numbers, or credit card numbers to impersonate someone else. The information may be used to obtain credit, merchandise, or services in the name of the victim or to provide the thief with false credentials. Identity fraud is the fastest-growing white-collar crime in many countries, especially in developed countries.

Mortgage Fraud

To obtain a mortgage for real estate acquisition by a private person, the person has to state his or her income. Before the financial crisis in 2008 in the US, it was determined that 60 percent of the applicants for the loans examined overstated their income by 50 percent or more. Often, borrowers and real estate professionals combined to engage in fraud for profit schemes. Such schemes exploited the defining characteristics of subprime lending such as 100 percent financing and weak underwriting standards. In an industry driven by commissions, lending officers were encouraged to participate in fraud schemes.

The more loans the lenders' sales representatives could originate, the more money they made. Mortgage brokers and individuals inside lending institutions thus had powerful incentives to join mortgage fraud schemes by adding dirt to the loan files. They were staging loan files to include false documents as well as ignoring obvious misrepresentations on loan documents.

Occupational Fraud

Most developed countries have experienced a number of occupational fraud cases in the last decade, including the Enron, WorldCom, Societe Generale, and the Parmalat frauds. Peltier-Rivest (2009) defines occupational fraud as the use of one's occupation for personal enrichment through the deliberate misuse or misapplication of the employing organization's resources or assets. Any fraud committed by an employee, a manager, executive, or by the owner of an organization where the victim is the organization itself may be considered occupational fraud, which is sometimes called internal fraud. Sometimes labelled financial statement fraud, inaccurate earnings figures may be used as a basis for performance bonuses.

Included in occupational fraud is basic company fraud. For example, when an employee fakes sickness to obtain paid sick leave, submits inflated overtime claims, or uses company equipment for an unauthorized purpose, which may be to operate a private business. Asset misappropriations may be cash or non-cash. Cash schemes include cash larceny, skimming, or fraudulent disbursements such as billing schemes, payroll fraud, cheque tampering, and expense reimbursement frauds. Non-cash schemes include theft of inventory, equipment, proprietary information, and securities.

Subsidy Crime

Subsidy crime pertains to criminal offences committed when government subsidies are granted. A person or a business might provide incorrect information when applying for government subsidies or use the subsidies contrary to intentions and agreements. A similar kind of fraud of the public is sundry frauds, where an example is illegal price fixing cartels or yearly fuel subsidy in Nigeria.

Theft Crime

Theft can be defined as the illegal taking of another person's, group's, or organization's property without the victim's consent.

Art Theft

Art theft is art crime involving theft by burglary, robbery, deception (frauds, fakes, forgery, and false attribution), and might involve money laundering. Hill (2008) suggests that the monetary value of stolen works of art is not as great as the value of art frauds, fakes, forgeries, dodgy attributions, and bogus provenance in the art, antiques, and antiquities world.

One kind of art theft is trophy art crime, where some violent criminals enjoy the self-esteem, self-regard, and self-indulgence they feel when committing high-profile art crimes at specific times, often when law enforcement resources are stretched. Some examples include (Hill 2008, 445):

- The theft of the original version of Edvard Munch's "Scream" stolen from the National Gallery in Oslo on the first day of the 1994 Winter Olympics in Lillehammer.
- The theft of Titian's *Rest on the Flight into Egypt* and two other sixteenth-century pictures from Longleat House, *Wiltshire on Twelfth Night*, January 6, 1995.
- The theft of the Ashmolean's only Cezanne in Oxford on Millennium Eve night 2000.
- The armed robbery at the Isabella Stewart Gardner Museum in Boston, Massachusetts, on the night of St. Patrick's Day 1990 in which several Rembrandts, a Vermeer, and other highly significant works of art were stolen.

The financial value of stolen art varies, as the market for such stolen goods is limited. Hill (2008) argues that money laundering through works of art is serious but more a matter of tax evasion rather than from the laundering of illicit drug profits.

Theft of Cash

For example, skimming occurs when cash is taken before it enters the books. Embezzlement involves direct breach of trust when someone entrusted with the cash diverts it for personal use. Lapping is a technique whereby the theft of cash or cheques is covered up by using later receipts so that the gap in funds is not noticed.

Identity Theft

A distinction can be made between identity fraud and identity theft. While identity fraud refers to actual misuse of obtained identifiers and engaging in unlawful activities committed by impersonating victims, identity theft refers to obtaining those identifiers of an identity holder by being a thief. Typically, identity theft is an enabler of identity fraud. Identity theft is the crime of acquiring another's personal information without their knowledge. Identity theft is the acquisition of sufficient data for one individual to successfully impersonate another. It involves securing pieces of an individual's personal information (for example, birth number, driver's licence, social security number) and using the information extracted from these forms of identification to impersonate the individual.

Identity theft combined with identity fraud is the unlawful use of another's personal identifying information. It involves financial or other personal information stolen with the intent of establishing another person's identity as the thief's own. It occurs when someone uses personally identifying information, like name, social security number, date of birth, government passport number, or credit card number without the owners' permission to commit fraud or other crimes. Identity theft is a behaviour that threatens the growth and development of economies worldwide and has been viewed as the crime of the new millennium. In their study, they found that states with more males, higher residential mobility, and more entertainment establishments are likely to have more identity theft complaints.

Intellectual Property Crime

Intellectual property crime is a serious financial concern for car manufacturers, luxury goods makers, media firms, and drug companies. Most alarmingly, according to Interpol (2009), counterfeiting endangers public health, especially in developing countries, where the World Health Organization estimates more than 60 percent of pharmaceuticals are fake goods.

Interpol (2009) launched a new database on international intellectual property crime, which was created to fill the void in seizure data collated by various international bodies and the private sector. Of 1,710 entities in the database, checks against other Interpol databases revealed links to credit card and currency counterfeiting; fraud; money laundering; theft; violent crimes; and trafficking in human beings, weapons, and drugs. This demonstrates the role of organized crime in large-scale counterfeiting and piracy.

Inventory Theft

This is stealing from a company.

Manipulation Crime

Manipulation can be defined as a means of gaining illegal control or influence over others' activities, means, and results.

Bankruptcy Fraud

Bankruptcy crime is criminal acts committed in connection with bankruptcy or liquidation proceedings. Bankruptcy fraud is committed by businesses or individuals, who conceal assets, mislead creditors, falsely claim bankruptcy, file multiple bankruptcy claims, or launch petition mills. A person filing for bankruptcy or a business that has gone into liquidation can hide assets after proceedings have been initiated, thereby preventing creditors from collecting their claims. Another example of bankruptcy crime is the inventory. Inventory is usually shipped to the enterprise premises. Afterward, it is transported to another enterprise premise, which is controlled by the same principals. There it is sold, and the profits are diverted to the principals. Normally, a corporate shield will be in place to hide the principals involved in the scheme.

Organized crime will take over a business not to keep it alive and healthy but to force the company into bankruptcy after making a quick cash profit. Individuals commit bankruptcy fraud by not disclosing or hiding assets from the trustee. For small businesses, this can be devastating. They are usually not able to recover the losses. For larger businesses, they pass the loss—which could take weeks, months, or even years to recover—on to other customers by raising their prices. The prime characteristic of bankruptcy fraud is the hiding or nondisclosure of assets. This leaves little or no means of recovery by creditors. This is called "bust out." Bust outs have become more prevalent in recent years, especially in high-inventory-turnover businesses. This crime usually requires identification of inventory purchased, sold, and "carted" off.

Bid Rigging

This occurs when a vendor is given an unfair advantage to defeat a competitor in an open tender for a given contract. A vendor may be provided with extra information to bid low but then raise more income through many variations to the set contract. This may be linked to the receipt of kickbacks.

Competition Crime

Competition crime is collaborating on and influencing prices, profits, and discounts as well as tender and market-sharing collaboration. The prohibition regulations in competition laws first of all target cartel collaboration where market participants in a particular industry collaborate in order to limit the competition. They may divide the market between themselves and agree what prices to charge their customers. Prices will be higher than if real competition prevailed in the market.

Computer Crime

This is defined as any violations of criminal law that involve knowledge of computer technology for their perpetration, investigation, or prosecution. The initial role of information and communication technology (ICT) was to improve the efficiency and effectiveness of organizations.

However, the quest of efficiency and effectiveness serves more obscure goals as fraudsters exploit the electronic dimension for personal profits. Computer crime is an overwhelming problem that has brought an array of new crime types. Examples of computer-related crimes include sabotage, software piracy, and stealing personal data. In computer crime terminology, the term *cracker* is typically used to denote a hacker with a criminal intent. No one knows the magnitude of the computer crime problem—how many systems are invaded, how many people engage in the practice or the total economic damage. The most economically damaging kinds of computer crime are denial-of-service attacks, where customer orders might be rerouted to another supplier.

Counterfeit Currency

Currency counterfeiting and money laundering have the potential to destabilize national economies and threaten global security as these activities are sometimes used by terrorists and other dangerous criminals to finance their activities or conceal their profits. The crime of counterfeiting currency is as old as money itself. In the past, nations had used counterfeiting as a means of warfare. The idea was to overflow the enemy's economy with fake banknotes so that the real value of the said money was reduced and thereby attacking the economy and general welfare of a society.

Cybercrime

Attacks on the cyber security infrastructure of business organizations can have several goals. One goal pursued by criminals is to gain unauthorized access to the target's sensitive information. Most businesses are vitally dependent on their proprietary information, including new product information, employment records, price lists, and sales figures. An attacker may derive direct economic benefits from gaining access to and/or selling such information or may inflict damage on an organization by impacting upon it. Once access has been attained, attackers can not only extract and use or sell confidential information, they can also modify or delete sensitive information, resulting in significant consequences for their targets.

Cybercrime and computer crime are both related to Internet crime. The Internet is a "double-edged sword" that provides many opportunities for individuals and organizations to develop. At the same time, the Internet has brought with it new opportunities to commit crime. Internet crime has become a global issue that requires full cooperation and participation of both developing and developed countries at the international level.

Extortion

Extortion is a criminal offence, which occurs when a person unlawfully obtains money, property or services from a person, entity, or institution through coercion. Coercion is the practice of compelling a person or forcing them to behave in an involuntary way. A common abuse of public authority in some countries relates to the enforcement of road traffic regulations (or other minor infractions) where informal on-the-spot fines (or bribes) are negotiated with the alleged offender, rather than pursuing a formal prosecution or other legal process. In extreme circumstances, this can be regarded by some as the normal way of doing business. Assessors may experience this first hand.

Ghost Employees

This is getting extra names on to a company payroll and diverting the funds to a bank account specifically set up for this scam. If an employee can stay on the payroll after having left the company, again extra funds can be obtained for a while.

Inflated Invoices

A company inflates its bills without agreement from the bill payer, who may be a customer. Conversely, an employee may arrange to pay a vendor more than is due in return for an unauthorized payment or some other gain. Similarly, travel and entertainment (subsistence) claims occur when claims are falsified, inflated, or there is basic abuse of the schemes. Also similar are misappropriation schemes—altering sales figures, writing off income that was actually received, obtaining blank purchase orders, amending documentation, diverting vendor discounts, and writing off balances are some examples here.

Money Laundering

This is an important activity for most criminal activity. Money laundering means the securing of the proceeds of a criminal act. The proceeds must be integrated into the legal economy before the perpetrators can use it. The purpose of laundering is to make it appear as if the proceeds were acquired legally, as well as disguising its illegal origins.

Money laundering takes place within all types of profit-motivated crime, such as embezzlement, fraud, misappropriation, corruption, robbery, distribution of narcotic drugs, and trafficking in human beings.

Money laundering has often been characterized as a three-stage process that requires (1) moving the funds from direct association with the crime; (2) disguising the trail to foil pursuit; and (3) making them available to the criminal once again with their occupational and geographic origins hidden from view. The first stage is the most risky one for the criminals since money from crime is introduced into the financial system. Stage 1 is often called the placement stage. Stage 2 is often called the layering stage, in which money is moved in order to disguise or remove direct links to the offence committed. The money may be channelled through several transactions, which could involve a number of accounts, financial institutions, companies, and funds, as well as the use of professionals such as lawyers, brokers, and consultants as intermediaries. Stage 3 is often called the integration stage, where a legitimate basis for asset origin has been created. The money is made available to the criminal and can be used freely for private consumption, luxury purchases, real estate investment, or investment in legal businesses. Money laundering has also been described as a five-stage process—placement, layering, integration, justification, and embedding.

Income Tax Crime

The failure to comply with national income tax laws is one of the most prevalent financial crimes in many countries. Tax evasion can be divided into three main categories—undeclared work/business, unlawful planning and adjustment of taxes, and exploitation of ambiguities or alleged "loopholes" in the legislation so as to obtain improper tax advantages.

Tax avoidance is the act of taking advantage of legally available opportunities to minimize one's tax liability. Individuals and legal entities tend to choose a tax alternative, which will incur the least income tax liability. This is known as tax planning that is taking place within certain legal boundaries. However, tax-planning strategies encounter boundaries that are sometimes difficult to identify. For example, there is a gray area between tax avoidance, which is legal tax saving and tax evasion, which is illegal.

Tax evasion is defined as the wilful attempt to defeat or circumvent the tax law in order to illegally reduce one's tax liability. Tax evasion is illegal while tax avoidance is a legal approach to saving taxes. In many legislation regions, the crime of tax evasion requires a positive action. A mere passive neglect of the statutory duty is then insufficient to establish violation. Acts such as submitting incorrect statements of accounts, making false entries or alterations, or false books or records, destruction of books and records, concealment of assets or covering up sources of income constitute tax evasion. A special kind of tax fraud is value added tax (VAT) fraud.

Corruption Crime

Corruption is defined as the giving, requesting, receiving, or accepting of an improper advantage related to a position, office, or assignment. The improper advantage does not have to be connected to a specific action or to not-doing this action. It will be sufficient if the advantage can be linked to a person's position, office, or assignment. An individual or group is guilty of corruption if they accept money or money's worth for doing something that he is under a duty to do anyway, that he is under a duty not to do, or to exercise a legitimate discretion for improper reason. Corruption is to destroy or pervert the integrity or fidelity of a person in his discharge of duty. It is to induce to act dishonestly or unfaithfully; it is to make venal; and it is to bribe.

Corruption involves behaviour on the part of officials in the public or private sectors in which they improperly and unlawfully enrich themselves and/or those close to them or induce others to do so by misusing the position in which they are placed. Corruption covers a wide range of illegal activity such as kickbacks, embezzlement, and extortion. Money laundering as well in his definition of corruption. The notion of corruption may be classified as sporadic or systemic corruption, bureaucratic or political corruption, grand or petty corruption, and active and passive corruption.

From an economic perspective, corruption is generally defined as the misuse of position of authority for private or personal benefit based on external influences. The external influence supplies benefits to solve a problem. Typically, a problem is solved by providing benefits to persons in positions of authority. Corruption when applying the value shop configuration reflects rational, self-interested behaviour by the principal using its discretion to direct allocations to other social actors who offer rewards in return for favourable discretionary treatment. Corruption is a response to situations that present opportunities for gain and the discretionary power to appropriate that gain.

Bribery

Bribery is corruption conducted to achieve a favourable treatment. For example, a criminal entrepreneur is dependent on a favourable treatment to succeed in organized crime. An organization of corrupt individuals is a behavioural phenomenon, while a corrupt organization is a top-down phenomenon in which a group of organization members undertake corrupt actions. Corrupt actions are carried out by the dominant coalition, organizational elites or top management team, directly or through their subordinates to the benefit of the organization.

Deciding to bribe is the result of a problem-solving activity. Bribery activity can involve organizations in their home country or abroad and can involve the local or foreign governments with which organizations might interact. Bribery activity differs on the basis of who is supplying as opposed to demanding the bribes and whether public or private sector institutions are involved.

Kickbacks

An employee with influence over who gets a particular contract is able and willing to obtain something for assisting the prospective contractor. Likewise, bribes may be paid to inspectors to turn a blind eye to substandard goods coming into a loading dock. If bribes do not work, the dedicated fraudster may well turn to blackmail and pose threats. Modern criminal justice systems try to ensure that victims of crime are compensated for injuries and losses suffered at the hands of the defendant.

Organizational Corruption

Organizational corruption, which Lange (2008) defines as the pursuit of interests by organizational actors through the intentional misdirection of organizational resources or perversion of organizational routines, might ultimately impede the organization's ability to accomplish its legitimate purpose and may threaten its very survival.

Public Corruption

This is the abuse of entrusted power by political leaders for private gain. The corrosive effect of corruption undermines all efforts to improve governance and foster development. Corruption is just as much an economic problem as it is a political and social one since it is a "cancer" that burdens the poor in developing countries (Berkman et al. 2008, 125):

> *Corruption works to undermine development projects in three primary ways. First, the world's poor often do not receive the full benefit of development aid because as much as 10, 20, 30 and even higher percentages of development loans are siphoned*

off—often in the form of bribes—by corrupt actors, such as government officials, contractors, and in rare cases, by employees of international organizations. Bribe payers in turn short-change the project by, for example, using substandard materials or performing below specification, in order to pay these bribes.

Second, even though aid recipients may consequently receive only a fraction in benefits from every dollar or euro spent for development aid because of corruption, they nonetheless have to pay back the full amount of the development loan, often with interest. The resulting debt burdens placed on the world's poor stifle any chance they may have of freeing themselves from the vexing cycle of poverty and debt. Worse still, the poor in developing nations grow cynical of international organizations that lend money to corrupt leaders while providing little or no oversight to ensure these loans are used for the purposes intended.

Third, corruption leads to donor fatigue. Taxpayers from donor countries, along with their elected representatives responsible for approving development aid budgets, are increasingly skeptical that development projects are being effectively implemented. Pleas from international aid agencies that more aid is needed for development projects or famine relief are increasingly falling on the deaf ears of taxpayers, who perceive that international organizations either ignore, or do little to stop, the corruption that makes a mockery of international aid.

Public corruption is found all over the world. Corruption can play an important role in the building up of criminal organizations. Criminal entrepreneurs may expand their illegal activities by bribing local officials.

Reflection Menu

1. There are three factors that are present in financial crimes, EXCEPT:
   a. something of value must be present
   b. an opportunity to take something of value without being detected must be present
   c. there must be a motivating factor for a perpetrator to be willing to commit the offense
   d. there must be a perpetrator who is willing to commit the offense

2. The illegal taking of another person's property without the victim's consent is a _____ Fraud.
   a. Corruption
   b. Theft
   c. Manipulation

3. A means of gaining illegal control or influence over others' activities, means, and results is referred to as
   a. Fraud
   b. Corruption
   c. Theft
   d. Manipulation

4. Art theft is art crime involving all of the following EXCEPT
   a. theft by burglary, robbery, deception
   b. frauds, fakes, forgery, and false attribution
   c. theft by burglary, robbery, money laundering
   d. frauds, fakes, forgery, and theft

(For the answers, please turn to Appendix A)

3 Why People Commit Financial Crimes

Introduction

Research shows that anyone can commit financial crime or fraud. Financial crime perpetrators usually can't be distinguished from other people on the basis of demographic or psychological characteristics. Most financial crime perpetrators have profiles that look like those of other honest people. Several years ago, a study was conducted to determine the physical and behavioral characteristics of financial crime perpetrators. In this study, fraud perpetrators were compared with (1) prisoners incarcerated for property offenses and (2) a sample of noncriminal college students. The personal backgrounds and psychological profiles of the three groups were compared. The results indicated that incarcerated fraud perpetrators were very different from other incarcerated prisoners.

Financial crime or fraud perpetrators were better educated, more religious, less likely to have criminal records, less likely to have abused alcohol, and considerably less likely to have used drugs. They were also in better psychological health. They enjoyed more optimism, self-esteem, self-sufficiency, achievement, motivation, and family harmony than other property offenders. Financial crime or fraud perpetrators also seemed to express more social conformity, self-control, kindness, and empathy than other property offenders. Individuals involved in financial crime or fraud are typically people just like you and me but have compromised their integrity and become entangled in financial crime or fraud.

It is important to understand the characteristics of financial crime or fraud perpetrators because they appear to be very much like people who have traits that organizations look for in hiring employees, seeking out customers and clients, and selecting vendors. This knowledge helps us to understand that (1) most employees, customers, vendors, and business associates and partners fit the profile of fraud perpetrators and are capable of committing fraud, and (2) it is impossible to predict in advance which employees, vendors, clients, customers, and others will become dishonest. In fact, when fraud does occur, the most common reaction by those around the fraud is denial. Victims cannot believe that trusted colleagues or friends have behaved dishonestly.

The Fraudsters

Personality Traits of the Fraudsters

Under this title, we will examine the characteristic features of people who commit or are likely to commit fraud on businesses. However, it does not imply that the person with these traits will definitely commit fraud. These characteristics should hopefully guide investigative auditors to detect the fraud.

- *Gender.* A survey by Association of Certified Fraud Examiners (ACFE) with 2,000 fraudsters revealed many characteristics of fraudsters. According to this survey, three out of four of the people who commit fraud in businesses are male. This difference is explicit also in the monetary value of the fraud.
- *Marital status.* It is shown that the number of married employees who attempt to commit fraud is higher than unmarried employees. With respect to the amount of fraud, the difference is 1–3. In addition, many of them have children and a happy marriage.

- *Education status.* Generally, as the level of education increases, the number and amount of the fraud also increase. The amount of the fraud is much higher, especially with employees who had received good education.
- *IQ level.* Employees with higher IQ levels or those claiming to be so have a higher level of desire to commit fraud. The underlying reason of this situation is that this kind of people challenges the internal control structures and security systems of business they work in and satisfies themselves by breaking through them.
- *Age level.* Employees of any age could attempt to commit fraud, but the number and amount of the fraud are higher with older people. The number of fraud older people commit is twenty-eight times higher than those young people commit.
- *Working conditions.* Generally, employees who come earliest and leave latest commit fraudulent activities more. Especially employees who present their unfinished jobs as an excuse and want to work alone until late hours of the night have higher probability of committing fraud. Moreover, it is estimated that many of the managers who are caught as a result of fraudulent activities do not take a leave unless they have to. The reason is predicted that they think whoever is assigned to replace them when they are away would discover and report the irregularities before their return.
- *Position at the business.* Any person working in the business has a probability to somewhat commit fraud. However, studies indicate that with respect to the amount of fraud, employees at managerial positions are by far ahead of other employees. When employees have a trustworthy position, they are monitored less; this is considered as the underlying reason of the preceding fact. Moreover, due to their position, they are in a better position to understand the entity's internal control structures and gaps in them and are thus able to conduct fraudulent activity more easily. Unfortunately, the first reaction of many fraud victims is, "I could never expect him/her to do that."

- *Relations outside of business.* Another indicator is the level of relations employees have with third parties of the business. When an employee becomes very intimate with people buying/selling goods and services from the business, conditions become congenial for fraud to be perpetrated.

Who Commits Fraud? Different Types of Fraudsters

Fraudsters usually fall into one of three categories:

- Preplanned fraudsters, who start out from the beginning intending to commit fraud. These can be short-term players, like many who use stolen credit cards or false social security numbers, or can be longer-term, like bankruptcy fraudsters and those who execute complex money-laundering schemes.
- Intermediate fraudsters, who start off honest but turn to fraud when times get hard or when life events, such as irritation at being passed over for promotion or the need to pay for care for a family member, change the normal mode.
- Slippery-slope fraudsters, who simply carry on trading even when, objectively, they are not in a position to pay their debts. This can apply to ordinary traders or to major business people

In 2007, KPMG carried out research on the *Profile of a Fraudster* (KPMG survey) using details of fraud cases in Europe, India, the Middle East, and South Africa. The ACFE carried out similar research on frauds committed in the US. These surveys highlight the following facts and figures in relation to fraudsters:

- Perpetrators are typically college educated male.
- Most fraudsters are aged between thirty-six and fifty-five.
- The majority of frauds are committed by men.
- Median losses caused by men are twice as great as those caused by women.

- A high percentage of frauds are committed by senior management (including owners and executives).
- Losses caused by managers are generally more than double those caused by employees.
- Average losses caused by owners and executives are nearly twelve times those of employees.
- Longer-term employees tend to commit much larger frauds.
- Fraudsters most often work in the finance department, operations/sales, or as the CEO.

The ACFE report also found that the type of person committing the offence depends on the nature of the fraud being perpetrated. Employees are most likely to be involved in asset misappropriation, whereas owners and executives are responsible for the majority of financial statement frauds. Of the employees, the highest percentage of schemes involved those in the accounting department. These employees are responsible for processing and recording the organization's financial transactions and so often have the greatest access to its financial assets and more opportunity to conceal the fraud.

The Fraud Triangle and Diamond

Why Do People Commit Fraud?

When business frauds are analyzed, it is ascertained that three components come together when committing the white-collar crime. These are pressure, opportunity, and justification that constitute the "fraud triangle." Components of the fraud triangle are similar to the fuel, spark, and oxygen that together cause fire. When the three come together, inevitably, fire breaks out. Looking from the fraudster's perspective, it is necessary to take account of

1. motivation of potential offenders;
2. conditions under which people can rationalise their prospective crimes away;

3. opportunities to commit crime(s);
4. perceived suitability of targets for fraud;
5. technical ability of the fraudster;
6. expected and actual risk of discovery after the fraud has been carried out;
7. expectations of consequences of discovery (including non-penal consequences such as job loss and family stigma, proceeds of crime confiscation, and traditional criminal sanctions); and
8. actual consequences of discovery.

A common model that brings together a number of these aspects is the fraud triangle and fraud diamond model. Fraud triangle model is built on the premise that fraud is likely to result from a combination of three factors: (1) perceived incentives/Pressures, (2) perceived opportunities, and (3) rationalization of fraudulent behavior. Fraud diamond model adds fourth variable "capabilities" to the three factors of fraud triangle.

Image

Pressure

Pressure (or incentive or motivation) refers to something that has happened in the fraudster's personal life that creates a stressful need that motivates him to steal. Usually that motivation centers on some financial strain, greed, or need, but it could be the symptom of other types of pressures. Beyond the realm of competitive and economic survival, other motives for fraud include (1) nonfinancial pressures, such as the expectation for good results at work, the imposition of unachievable goals, or the need to cover up a poorly performed job. (2) Social and political survival provide incentives in the form of egocentric and ideological motives. (3) Psychotic—it cannot be explained in terms of rational behaviour, but it involve a pathological liar, the professional confidence man, and the kleptomaniac.

Pressure factors could be gathered into three groups:

1. Pressures with financial content

   Pressures with financial contents generally show up when people are in need of cash.

   These pressures could be classified as below:
   • Itching palm and greediness
   • Desire to live well
   • High amounts of personal debts
   • High amounts of health expenditures
   • Unexpected financial needs

The very first reason of employee fraud is that they are poor due to lower income they receive and want to live under better conditions. Pressures with financial content could come into view in the long term as well as in the short term. An employee who has been working in business for a number of years could commit fraud for some reason.

2. Pressures stemming from bad habits

Pressures arising from bad habits have attributes related with pressures with financial content. Being a gambler, drug or alcohol addict, and keen on nightlife are among the several reasons causing fraud. This kind of habit is accepted as the worst kind of factors motivating fraud. There are many examples of women employees committing fraud to buy drug or alcohol for their children or husbands or of managers who are very successful in their professional lives but commit fraud because of their gambling ambition.

3. Pressures related with job

Pressures related with the job could be explained as being dissatisfied with the job, the idea of an unfair attitude, not getting promoted when expected, having worked with lower wage, or not being admired by supervisors.

Opportunity

Fraudsters always have the knowledge and opportunity to commit the fraud, and the fraudster must believe the fraud can be committed with impunity. Prior research studies such as the Association of Certified Fraud Examiners' Report to the Nation (RTTNs) show that employees and managers with a long tenure in a company know quite well where the weaknesses are in the internal controls and have gained sufficient knowledge of how to commit the crime successfully. Absent or ineffective controls, lack of supervision, or inadequate segregation of duties may provide such opportunities. The main factor in opportunity therefore is internal controls.

Fraud is more likely in companies where there is a weak internal control system, poor security over company property, little fear of exposure and likelihood of detection, or unclear policies with regard to acceptable behaviour. Research has shown that some employees are totally honest, some are totally dishonest, but that many are swayed by opportunity. When motivation is coupled with such opportunities, the potential for fraud is increased.

The control structure of the business and fraud has an inverse correlation. The most effective way of reducing employee frauds is to establish an "internal control system."

The important points when establishing the system are given below:

- A healthy internal control environment
- A proper accounting system
- Control procedures that operate effectively

Other factors that provide employees with the opportunity to commit fraud are as following:

- Weak moral policies
- Undisclosed contracts made with third parties and partners
- Incapability to assess the quality of the job employees performed
- Absence of a well-disciplined environment in which fraudsters will be punished
- Weakness of the information flow among employees within the business
- Ignorance, indifference, and inabilities of top management
- Lack of healthy audit works

When there is a situation where environment to punish the fraudster is absent because of the concerns such as loss of prestige and counter threat, the feeling of "you can get away with it" will be evoked among employees; thus, the business will be exposed to frauds.

Rationalization

Rationalization is the process by which an employee determines that the fraudulent behavior is "okay" in her or his mind. Many excuses could serve as a rationalization; it could be

1. Social purposes—where the fraudster does not actually keep the stolen funds or assets but uses them for social purposes (e.g., to fund an animal clinic for stray animals).
2. Fair treatment—where the fraudster believed that he deserve a raise or better treatment.
3. Borrowing—where the fraudster steals from employers but mentally convinces himself that he will repay it.
4. Benign—where the fraudster believed that it hurts no one so that makes the theft benign.

Many people obey the law because they believe in it and/or they are afraid of being shamed or rejected by people they care about if they are caught. However, some people may be able to rationalise fraudulent actions as

- necessary—especially when done for the business,
- harmless—because the victim is large enough to absorb the impact,
- justified—because "the victim deserved it" or "because I was mistreated."

Management has the most control over the opportunity portion of the fraud triangle by limiting access to assets and put controls in place that ensure monitoring of systems and people. Also, motivation can be constrained by management, and the best way to reduce "needs" is by paying employees fairly (to reduce perceived financial burdens) and by creating performance systems that are reasonable (not requiring job performance beyond what is realistic). Rationalization is the most dangerous piece of the fraud triangle because it is the one that companies have the least control over. It is nearly impossible for management to eliminate the rationalization piece because they can't control the minds of employees. Management has no way of knowing what lies an employee may tell himself in order to justify fraud in his mind, so there is virtually no way of counteracting the lies.

At the macro level, in order to overcome these justifying excuses, business should explain ethic rules to employees, inform them that fraudsters would definitely be penalized, establish moral code in the organization, and provide training on them.

Capabilities

Wolf and Hermanson (2004) introduced the fraud diamond model where they presented another view of the fraud triangle (why do people commit fraud). Many frauds would not have occurred without the right person with right capabilities implementing the details of the fraud.

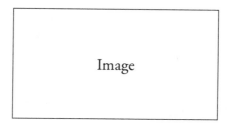

Six traits often associated with the capability element that Wolfe and Hermanson believe are essential in the personality of the fraudster.

1. *Positioning.* The person's position or function within the organization may provide the ability to create or exploit an opportunity for fraud. A person in a position of authority has more influence over particular situations or the environment.

2. *Intelligence and creativity.* The fraudster is smart enough to understand and exploit internal control weaknesses and to use position, function, or authorized access to the greatest advantage.

3. *Ego.* The individual must have a strong ego and great confidence he will not be detected. The common personality types include someone who is driven to succeed at all costs, self-absorbed, self-confident, and often narcissistic. According to the Diagnostic and Statistical Manual of Mental Disorders, narcissistic personality disorder is a pervasive pattern of grandiosity, a need for admiration, and a lack of empathy for others. Individuals with this disorder believe they are superior or unique, and they are likely to have inflated views of their own accomplishments and abilities.

4. *Coercion.* A fraudster can coerce others to commit or conceal fraud. An individual with a persuasive personality can more successfully convince others to go along with the fraud or look the other way.

5. *Deceit*. Successful fraud requires effective and consistent lies. In order to avoid detection, the individual must be able to lie convincingly and must keep track of the overall story.

6. *Stress*. The individual must be able to control their stress, as committing the fraudulent act and keeping it concealed can be extremely stressful.

Indicators of Financial Crimes Activities

What Are Fraud Indicators?

Within an organization, internal fraud can be perpetrated by any employee from the most junior to the most senior. Where fraud is perpetrated from outside the organization, it can be with the assistance of an employee or "insider." There are a number of recognised warning signs or "red flags" that *may* indicate that an employee is engaged in a fraudulent activity. These indicators can be a powerful part of risk assessment when combined with other relevant information.

Why Are They Important?

Internal frauds are a big issue for organizations and are usually triggered by one of four situations:

- *Opportunistic crime*. Employees commit fraud for their own benefit. This may be entirely opportunistic or carefully planned. There are likely to be a number of possible motives.
- *Lack of a corporate ethic*. In some organizations, low-level fraud, such as the inflation of expenses claims, may appear to be condoned by both employer and employee.
- *The recruited criminal*. Some individuals seek employment (often in the financial sector) with the deliberate intention of defrauding their employer or gathering intellectual property.

70

- *Employee intimidation.* Organised crime groups are increasingly involved in the intimidation of staff to directly participate in frauds or to provide information on customer accounts or internal procedures in order to assist other attempts. A common threat is the harming of family and friends. Employees who have succumbed to an approach from a third party, provided information and accepted a fee in return often feel they have been "bought for life." Fraud indicators should help to identify these triggers, which should then be addressed as part of a robust anti-fraud strategy.

"Red Flag" Indicators

There are a number of warning signs that can indicate that there may be a problem within your business. These should not be taken alone as evidence that fraud is occurring within the organization; there may be other legitimate explanations for the occurrence of these indicators. Fraud indicators are inherently interrelated. However, for ease of reference, they have been grouped together below under umbrella themes. This list is not exhaustive.

Behavioral

- Employees who consistently work longer hours than their colleagues for no apparent reason
- Employees who are reluctant to take holidays and/or time off
- Employees who are excessively secretive in relation to their work
- Employees known by others to be under duress for personal reasons
- Employees with a sudden change of lifestyle and/or social circle
- Employees under apparent stress without identifiable pressure

71

- Employees who are aggressive or defensive when challenged and/or controlling of certain colleagues
- Employees who are subject to complaints and/or tend to break the rules
- Employees who delay providing information or who provide different answers to different people
- Employees who ask to defer internal audits or inspections to "properly prepare"
- Employees with new and unusual relationships with other individuals or departments within the organization
- Employees who request significant detail about proposed internal audit scopes or inspections
- Excessively high or low staff turnover and/or new employees resigning quickly

Financial

- Cash-only transactions
- Poorly reconciled cash expenses or customer accounts
- Rising costs with no explanation or that are not commensurate with an increase in revenue.
- Large volume of refunds to customers
- Unusually large inventories
- Unusual transactions or inter-account transfers (even for small amounts)
- Remuneration disproportionately linked to activities such as sales
- Employees known by others to be under external financial pressure
- Employees who appear to make a greater than normal number of mistakes, especially where these lead to financial loss through cash or account
- Employees with unexplained sources of wealth.
- Employees with competing or undeclared external business interests.

- Employees who submit inconsistent and/or unreasonable expense claims.
- Employees at the highest level of performance (e.g., sales) where there might be a concern that they are achieving this through suspect activity.

Procedural

- Employees making procedural or computer-system enquiries inconsistent or not related to their normal duties
- New employees with knowledge of industry procedures but no such experience disclosed on their CV
- Prospective employees who are reluctant to provide full background information or who provide inaccurate or inconsistent information
- Key managers with too much hands-on control
- Insufficient oversight/audit applied
- An unusual number of customer complaints
- Customers or suppliers insisting on dealing with just one individual
- Managers who avoid using the purchasing department
- Tendering to one supplier only or to the same suppliers
- Lack of transparency
- Poor engagement with corporate governance philosophy
- Too much delegation by senior managers without proper review procedures

Reflection Menu

1. Most financial crime perpetrators have profiles that look like those of other honest people. TRUE [ ] FALSE [ ]
2. Components of the fraud triangle are similar to the fuel, spark, and oxygen that together cause fire. TRUE [ ] FALSE [ ]

3. Management has the less control over the opportunity portion of the fraud triangle by limiting access to assets TRUE[ ] FALSE [ ]

4. Pressure factors in fraud triangle model include the following EXCEPT
   a. Pressures stemming from bad habits
   b. Pressures related with job
   c. Pressures with financial content
   d. Pressures related to needs

5. Attribute of financial crime or fraud perpetrators include the following EXCEPT
   a. They were better educated and more religious.
   b. They are less likely to have criminal records.
   c. They are less likely to have abused alcohol and considerably less likely
   d. to have used drugs.
   e. All the above.
   f. None of the above.

6. Which of the following is not a category of fraudsters
   a. Pre-planned fraudsters, intermediate fraudsters
   b. Pre-prepared fraudsters, intermediate fraudsters
   c. Intermediate fraudsters, slippery-slope fraudsters
   d. Pre-planned fraudsters, slippery-slope fraudsters

7. Which of the following will not trigger internal fraud in an organization?
   a. Opportunistic crime
   b. Motivational crime
   c. Lack of a corporate ethic
   d. The recruited criminal
   e. Employee intimidation

8. Which six traits often associated with the capability element of the personality of the fraudster?
   a. Positioning, intelligence, creativity, ego and coercion, deceit, stress
   b. Positioning, intelligence and creativity, ego, coercion, deceit, stress
   c. Positioning, intelligence, creativity, ego, coercion, deceit, and stress
   d. Positioning, intelligence, creativity, ego, coercion and deceit, stress

9. Which of the following are excuses for rationalization?
   a. social purposes, fair treatment, borrowing, and benign
   b. social purposes, bad treatment, borrowing, and benign
   c. social purposes, good treatment, borrowing, and benign
   d. social purposes, fair treatment, necessary, borrowing, and benign

(For the answers, please turn to Appendix A.)

4 Investigative Techniques in Financial Crimes

Investigative Techniques

Observing Rights and Maintaining Staff Morale

An investigation into employee fraud delves into the activities of people implicated by the evidence gathered. These people may be witnesses, suspects, or just those who have information that may assist the investigators. Employees are generally required to cooperate with an internal investigation and may be asked questions about their movements, work, views, and anything else that are relevant. At times, little or no information is available on the actual terms of reference for the investigation, and most of the information obtained by the investigators is deemed confidential. The inquiries are often done with a great deal of secrecy.

Every individual has constitutional rights that supersede all other legal provisions and must be observed. Breach of these rights means that any evidence obtained inappropriately is likely to be dismissed by the trial judge. Not only is it best practice anyway to observe employee rights, but also, it also ensures that the investigation is not ruled out of bounds when the case comes to trial.

What About Evidence?

Fraud investigations are primarily about gathering evidence. The term *evidence* is somewhat abused in today's society but generally means compelling material that would convince a reasonable person. The objectives of an investigation may include obtaining evidence of past, present, and future crimes and working out who did what and why and when and possibly how (the modus operandi).

The state of the evidence is crucial, as a case may go before a grand jury to see if there is probable cause to believe that an offense has been committed. The grand jury may decide to indict the person in question, after which an arrest warrant may be issued. All of this is based on a consideration of the available evidence. *Evidence* is anything that can be presented to the courts to prove a case to the satisfaction of a jury. Legal evidence tends to prove or disprove any facts in question, and it is these facts that are argued in the court or at an internal staff disciplinary hearing.

Types of Evidence

The evidence obtained during an investigation may be directly derived from the fraud, or it may be circumstantial. There are many and varied sources of evidence, including the following:

- *Witness statements.* These are generally acceptable unless the witness has been impeached because of bias, conviction of a felony, or for making inconsistent remarks.
- *Circumstantial evidence relating to unaccounted income.* This is interesting because of the presumption that such income is from unrecorded and fraudulent activities. An analysis of income can support a claim that the suspect is in receipt of illicit income. The person's assets and liabilities are established along with income from official sources, less known expenses. The difference between the net income from known sources and actual income is income from unknown sources, and the inference from this fact is used to support the case against the defendant.
- *Financial reports on the suspect.* These may be obtained from a company that specializes in providing this type of information. Investigative consumer reports involve a great

deal of research, such as questioning friends, neighbors, and associates to form a view of the person's reputation and way of life. These are generally not admissible unless the suspect has previously agreed to this type of research.

- *Physical evidence.* This may consist of maps, photographs, and actual objects and is sometimes called *real evidence.*
- *Documentary evidence.* This type of evidence is varied and includes things such as invoices, computer printouts, letters, the contents of files, and legal documents.
- *Financial reports and operational data from the company that has been derived from normal business processing.*
- *Demonstrative evidence.* The investigators may compile evidence for the court, perhaps in the form of a written report on the case created by the team of investigators.
- *Analytical data.* The investigators may carry out analyses to assist their case, which may then be presented to the court as evidence. If a cash count is made and analyzed to show that the employee in question had been under recording sums of money over a defined period, this schedule could become a court exhibit. If the analysis contains any errors at all, it may cast a shadow of doubt over the entire case. Data mining of (for example) refunds per supervisor, amount, and customer can be used to identify strange relationships, but again, each suspicious item must be checked to provide evidence of a fraud.
- *Testimonials.* These can be derived from interviews and are made by witnesses under oath. Interviewing is dealt with later on.
- *Secondary evidence.* Whereas original documents may be seen as primary evidence, certified copies of documents, with a suitable explanation of why the originals are not available, may be accepted by the courts.

Interviewing

The best way to find out something is to ask someone in the know. This rule applies to all types of investigations, including work relating to employee fraud. An interview is a formal exchange of information through a series of structured questions and answers. The interviewer is in charge of the situation and should retain control over the way the communication is carried out and should use clear questioning to secure information that fulfills the objective of the interview. When starting a fraud investigation, interviewees may be divided into distinct categories, which may change as the investigation proceeds:

Representatives of management. In many cases, top management will have called in the investigators to look into a particular irregularity. These managers are responsible for the systems and controls that have been breached during commission of the fraud; interviews with them will focus on finding out about the system and how the fraud was perpetrated.

Witnesses and potential witnesses to the fraud. Most of the interviewing will be of people who can provide direct information that supports the investigation. Much of this information will constitute formal evidence that is forwarded to the police department involved in the investigation. Witnesses are interviewed with a view to providing evidence in the form of signed statements; any material attached to their statements will be included as exhibits. A person may start out as a witness but end up a suspect as the weight of evidence starts to point in his or her direction.

People with general background information. Another group of interviewees consists of people who have background material. If the fraud involves people who are not employed by the organization appearing on the payroll (ghost employees), the personnel manager may be interviewed to find out how newcomers get onto the payroll. Meanwhile, the payroll manager may be a key witness against a member of payroll staff who have decided to put nonexistent people into the system.

Experts, specialists, and third parties. Investigators may need to interview various experts who have been called in to form a view on matters crucial to the case.

The suspect. This person tends to come last in any list of interviewees; the usual scenario is to present the suspect with the evidence gathered during the investigation and ask for an explanation. The suspects may make a formal confession, if this is seen as appropriate, or dispute the facts presented. Alternatively, they may refuse to cooperate or simply lie. They may also offer an irrefutable explanation that immediately clears all allegations against them. Some suspects become too emotional to continue and ask to be excused from the interview.

Nonverbal Communication

Most communication between two people occurs nonverbally. If there is a conflict between what is being said and what is being conveyed through unspoken signals, most will believe the nonverbal signals. A good understanding of nonverbal communication (NVC) allows the interviewer to probe difficult areas to explore more sensitive topics and to follow up answers that may be concealing the truth. The conversation can move from the official agenda to the real agenda that lies underneath the surface. Changes in demeanor, language, tone, facial expressions, or anything else may give a clue that there is something more behind a one-word denial. Probing these and providing a platform for the truth is one way of getting to the whole truth. There is an entire range of NVC, including:

Spatial factors. The physical distance that is maintained between interviewer and respondent can be determined by cultural factors. Think about the implications of invading the space of the respondent and the effect this may have on the proceedings. The position of the desk and chairs can also create an impression of formality, informality, barriers, sharing secrets, and other concepts. The interviewer has a lot of control over this factor if the respondent is being questioned in a place chosen by the interviewer. There is more scope to observe body language when there is no desk between the two parties, and sitting side by side may encourage the sharing of secrets. Positioning can also depend on the expectations of those involved. It can be useful to be able to move closer to the respondent when an important issue is being explored. At the same time, ensure that there is no perception of harassment, coercion, or intimidation.

Body language. Gestures, stance, and the movement of limbs can be signals for the interviewer. A person may appear stiff when under pressure and adopt a more relaxed posture when answering questions that are easier to deal with. The same person may look toward the door when a question appears to close in on her and she feels trapped. A shift in posture may indicate agreement or disagreement with what is being said by the interviewer. Nervous reactions such as placing a hand over the mouth can mean that the words coming out are being pushed back in or filtered. Crossing legs and arms can be interpreted as a defensive gesture against a perceived threat from the interviewer.

Facial expressions. The eyes, eyebrows, mouth, and jaw muscles of the respondent can say a lot about the level of stress, anger, surprise, concern, uncertainty, and a whole array of different feelings being experienced at the time. The degree of eye contact can indicate comfort, discomfort, and avoidance.

Silences. Pauses, looking away, looking unsatisfied, not answering, and other uses of silence can be quite effective in getting the right information from the respondent. Silence can mean the interviewer is not happy with an answer or is simply thinking about the answer that has been given. It can also be used to drill down into the inner thoughts of the respondent—the so-called hidden agenda of truth.

Voice. The tone and pitch of the voice can suggest much. Stress, hesitation, and tremors can all indicate areas that should be probed further by the interviewer.

Language. The words used can give us a clue as to the thoughts behind the answers. Some argue that people distance themselves from subjects that incriminate them or reflect badly on them. For example, a purchase order that has been altered by someone in an office is referred to as the "office order" to suggest that everyone in the office had access to it and so anyone could have altered it.

Other Investigative Techniques

The investigation team is in place, and the workforce may or may not know that the inquiry is happening. Meanwhile, the investigators may or may not have a suspect at this stage. We come now to the type of work that may be carried out by the investigators. The strategy for conducting the investigation will depend entirely on what is being investigated, with a key driver being the question, "What evidence do we need, and how do we get hold of it in such as way as to support the case in a reliable and robust manner?" Evidence was discussed earlier, but we need to list a few of the techniques for getting good evidence.

Analytical Review

A comparison of figures over various periods or between departments may turn up inconsistencies that can be examined in some detail. If the allegation is that expensive goods are disappearing from a particular branch and the stock figures are being forged to hide the fraud, the problem has to be investigated. The figures at the branch may not be reliable, although these will have to be tested at some stage. The movement of spending on inventory over time and as a ratio of sales may be studied. Discrepancies that cannot be explained can be investigated. If the branch in question has a different ratio of stock turnover to sales than other similar branches, then again, this can be explored further. Evidence from such a review is only circumstantial but can lead to more direct evidence of the actual fraud itself.

Surveillance

When an investigation is not yet public and no one has been suspended, surveillance becomes a possible technique. Surveillance is about structured observation of events so that, unknown to those involved in the fraud, good evidence may be secured as part of the investigation into the fraud. Covert operation is more complicated and can involve getting someone to infiltrate those involved in the scam to get inside information, again as evidence for the investigation. There can be much personal risk to the person who is acting undercover. Physical frauds, such as the unauthorized removal of goods, checks, equipment, and so on, are well suited to surveillance exercises, as are frauds that involve the association of two parties (for example, when kickbacks are being taken). If the removal of valuables can be observed, or an inappropriate liaison spotted, this helps in proving the fraud.

Examination of Audit Trails

Most fraud investigations involve a lot of paperwork. Frauds that abuse financial systems and attack funds as they are moved between accounts tend to leave a paper trail. There is a record of the underlying transactions that traces the movement from start to finish—the finish presumably being to an account controlled by the offenders or their associates. One technique is to use this trail to document the fraud as it progresses through the systems and display the interactions by employees, both innocent and those implicated in the loss. Trails can result from documents, computer interactions, phone records, attendance records, and anything else that traces the movement of people, information, transactions, and resources.

Document Analysis

Documents may be analyzed to determine whether they can be used as evidence of fraud. An invoice may be a forgery, seeking payment for goods or services that never existed. As part of the investigation, the invoice will be subjected to forensic examination to ascertain

- o how it was produced;
- o what equipment was used to produce it;
- o whether it contains any distinguishing marks, including fingerprints;
- o how it was processed;
- o what inside information was needed to undertake the fraud; and
- o what the details on the invoice can tell us.

Computerized documents can be examined using stylistics, where the style of the writer is determined and an assessment made of the likelihood that a document was written by a particular person.

Verification

Verification involves finding and checking out something. It can be applied to real assets to check that they exist and belong to the company. If the allegation is that an employee is running a private company using the employer's resources and contacts to gain business, the offices of this private company may be visited to verify that it does in fact exist.

Reconciliation

Accounting systems are designed to be in balance. As a transaction is made—say, a transfer of money from the company bankers to the company—the funds will be debited to the company's bank account and credited to the banker as payment received. These accounts will be in balance as funds moving around the organization and between external parties are properly accounted for. Regular reconciliations should be carried out to ensure that accounts balance. The amount in the bank account should agree with the bank statement, taking into account checks due to be paid and income due to be credited to arrive at a reconciled bank account. Fraud involving financial systems may throw off the real figures so that they fall out of balance. It is by carrying out reconciliation that the fraud may be discovered. *Lapping* is a type of fraud that involves timing differences in receipt and banking receipts to cover up the theft of an earlier receipt. Lapping can be isolated by analyzing the income for any timing differences.

Using Expert Witnesses

Witnesses give evidence in court in response to questions that they answer factually and are generally not allowed to express their opinion. An exception to this rule relates to evidence given by an expert. A forensic examination of documents may be commissioned to look for forgeries or alterations or even a DNA assessment of, for example, stamps that have been licked by the suspect; such tasks must be done by experts. Handwriting can be checked to assess the likelihood of a match with other known samples of writing. Photocopies can be checked for a match with a particular copying machine to establish important links. Experts are required to express a professional opinion on matters that fall under their area of expertise, and after having carried out their examination, they will issue a report and present this to the court as evidence. An alternative explanation may be presented by the defense's appointed expert, particularly when the matter is complicated. The experts are employed to apply special knowledge to the case. They should make sure that they consider the following matters:

- Experts work with the facts and should be able to form an opinion based on these facts.
- They should classify the evidence to support the facts, and this evidence should be properly handled and filed.
- The work carried out by the expert is subject to discovery and can be examined by the defense team.

When presenting evidence in court, the expert needs to make sure the answers are clear, concise, specific, considered, and free of jargon, and that a professional demeanor is retained even under rigorous cross-examination.

Third-Party Confirmation

Most evidence of employee fraud will come from within the organization. There are, however, times when we need to step outside and talk to third parties. In this case, an official statement obtained from the third party can be added to the store of evidence. In one fraud, a senior officer was accused of accepting excessive levels of free samples from a major vendor and making inappropriate procurement decisions on that basis. The vendor was happy to give official confirmation of the gifts it provided for the officer and correspondence on proposed new purchases on the basis that it wished to retain the company's business. When any external party provides information, that party should sign a formal statement cross-referenced to documents used as exhibits.

Data Interrogation

Investigators may make good use of computer interrogation as part of the investigation. There is readily available software that can be used against downloaded data to analyze, assess, and extract records that fit the criteria set by the interrogation exercise. The payables database may be searched for the year to look for all invoices that match the profile of suspect items set by the investigator. All items that match will be sorted and reported so that the supporting paperwork can be extracted and examined. It may be necessary to flag items going to a certain expenditure code or for certain types of spend items or for vendors with a certain contact cell phone number for careful scrutiny; the interrogation software may be used for this task. In fact, the investigation of any frauds that involve large financial systems may benefit from the use of data interrogations, including data mining.

Personal Profile

Another good technique that can be used to guide the investigation is personnel profiling. A database may be compiled from information relating to employees who are implicated in the fraud. A great deal of information can be extracted from internal and external sources, such as:

Internal sources	External sources
• Personnel • Payroll • Expense claims • Invoices paid • Phone logs • Computer logs • Staff performance reports • Documents authorized by the subject • Car parking permits and records • Correspondence • Phone messages • Office diaries (and automated calendars) • Fax messages • Internet searches and e-mails • Incoming mail (but watch out for mail fraud) • Desk searches • Searches of wastepaper baskets • Other internal databases and records	• City health departments • Tax authorities • Regulatory agencies • County registers of voters • County courts • Registered corporations • Professional bodies such as for accountants, doctors, and dentists • Credit rating bureaus • Federal inspector general • Securities and Exchange Commission • Dun and Bradstreet • Chambers of Commerce • Better Business Bureau • Interpol • National Crime Information Center • Western Union • State and national directories • Banks, via search warrants or subpoenas

Each state has legislation on what personal records may be maintained and rules on access restrictions and which records are public. Such statutes are usually a version of the federal Freedom of Information Act and Privacy Act. Armed with an abundance of information, it is possible to build a comprehensive profile of suspects, known associates, and any business contacts to be used to assist the investigation. The information may help ascertain whether the suspect is implicated in the fraud.

Informants

Another weapon for investigators is to employ informers to provide inside information on the scam and give insight into ways that it could be tackled. Some informers are motivated by the small amounts of money they receive for their information; others are driven by a desire for justice or status or simply a desire to deflect attention from their own questionable activities. The legal system frowns on inducement, although it is quite right to acknowledge the assistance of people who may be implicated on the periphery of the scam. There is an art to managing informants, especially when they may have somewhat undesirable lifestyles and are able to get close to the criminals. When a gang of career criminals are involved in, say, credit card fraud via the Internet, investigations can become very seedy. If investigators get too close to an informant, they can become implicated in crimes that they have knowledge of. If an informant comes to any harm, the investigators may share some responsibility. Complicated "sting" exercises using people placed in delicate situations must be left to the professionals, as they require a great deal of preparation.

The information provided by informants should be thoroughly checked out before it is placed in the file of evidence. Things can become even more difficult when the informant has broken laws in the pursuit of information. The final point to consider is whether the informant would make a good witness or whether he or she would have to attend a court hearing as a result of the investigation. This point is relevant to all investigations.

At times, good evidence is obtained through confidential sources and covert techniques. If the case comes to court, a decision has to be made on whether to continue and reveal those covert techniques and sources. If this point is not considered at an early stage, the case may have to be dropped because of important sensitivities. When selecting investigators to carry out a particular task, make sure the persons chosen will make competent and credible witnesses. If not, do not use them.

A Model for Investigations of Employee Fraud

Financial crime should be investigated in a way that suits the situation by people who can best carry out the work. In practice, it is possible to set some kind of procedure for carrying out such an investigation. This procedure for each individual fraud will be different. For employee frauds, whenever possible, the fourteen-stage procedure set out below may be applied.

Procedure for investigating employee for fraud or white-collar crime:

1. Allegation
2. Background research
3. Preliminary report
4. Investigation plan
5. Support
6. Definition of barriers
7. Strategy
8. Full investigation
9. Interim reports
10. Witness statements
11. Suspect interview
12. Final report
13. Action
14. Review

Allegation

Most employee frauds or white-collar crime come to light because of information provided by an informant, the suspicions of people working in the section that is affected, or reports of an actual unexplained loss. There is need for a process to capture all allegations and ensure that they are given due consideration. A document should be used to detail the essence of the allegation and record the decision on whether or not to investigate the matters alluded to. All allegations should be conveyed to a nominated person and recorded in a database of reported frauds. This starts the investigation process.

Background research

Having received an allegation, the next stage is to carry out some basic background work. The main question is whether there is a real problem. When there is a clear loss—say, a large amount of money that should be in the company pension fund appears to be missing—further action is required. A specific allegation against a member of staff will likewise have to be checked out. This stage of the investigation will indicate the scope and scale of the problem and whether a full-blown investigation should be launched.

Preliminary report

The next stage is to write a first report of the matter that will go to nominated parties for consideration. For example, an allegation of kickbacks on contracts is made to the purchasing manager and then passed on to the compliance officer or chief fraud advisor for consideration. After carrying out some basic checks, the compliance officer should prepare a preliminary report covering:

- Introduction—the allegation and any information on hand regarding the informant or suspicions.
- Work done—the basic checks made to substantiate the allegation.

- Conclusions—whether the allegation is well founded and initial checks are consistent with the reported problem.
- A recommendation—is there a need for an investigation? If so, the focus and resource implications of a decision to go ahead with further work.
- Police involvement—appropriate at this stage?

Chief fraud advisor and a high-level fraud panel will oversee any investigation. Whatever the format, there should be a formal procedure to approve a full investigation. The preliminary report should be presented to the fraud panel by the chief fraud advisor (or equivalent) and discussed in confidence in some detail, with formal minutes taken. Based on the findings to date, a decision should be made, taking into account the best interests of the company. Possible involvement of local law enforcement should always be on the agenda, and the decision should revolve around timing so that the police are approached when there is a good case for examination. The chief fraud advisor should be asked to put together an investigation plan to cover the initial work required to conduct the investigation.

Investigation plan

The fraud investigation will start to take shape with the formulation of a plan. The plan will be put together by the chief fraud advisor and cover items such as:

a. *The lead investigator.* Someone has to be in charge of the investigation, and this should be determined at the outset. It may be an appointed external specialist from a respected firm; if so, the contractual details must be properly organized. The chief fraud advisor should oversee the entire exercise and act as the liaison between the fraud panel and the lead investigator.

b. *The attorney.* For larger investigations, an attorney should be appointed to take charge of the work. This allows the attorney-client privilege to protect information from disclosure, at least for a while.

c. *The terms of reference.* A clear objective should be set for the investigation. The investigation should be conducted in line with the fraud policy and standards for this type of work. An organization that sets a clear procedure for conducting employee fraud investigations, and subsequently ignores that procedure, is heading for major problems.

d. *Reporting lines.* It is a good idea to set up formal reporting lines early, at the start of the investigation. The potential audience for a large employee fraud includes:

- Chief executive officer
- Chief financial officer
- Chief internal auditor
- Chief personnel officer
- Chief fraud advisor
- Compliance officer
- External auditor
- Shareholders
- Director for the area affected

- Company attorney
- Investigators

The more people who know about the fraud and the investigation, the more chance there is that unauthorized persons—even the fraudster—will find out that an investigation has begun.

Support

Building on the defined reporting lines established earlier, the support infrastructure for the planned investigation has to be made clear. Several roles should be clearly defined, including those of:

CEO. The chief officer will want to see the fraud dealt with efficiently and will approve a budget for the project and ensure that it is properly spent.

Director for the area where the fraud occurred. We have argued that executive responsibility for managing the risk of fraud lies with management. One way to do this is to make the relevant director responsible for the way the fraud is handled. The director may well join the fraud panel and make executive decisions as a result of the work done and reports issued by the investigators. All this is on the understanding that the director is in no way implicated in the problem through direct involvement or indirect negligence.

Fraud panel. Relevant key officers will sit on the panel, review the progress of the investigation, and make executive decisions based on recommendations from the investigating team. Personnel, legal representatives, the chief internal auditor, and a representative from the CEO's office may sit on the panel whenever it meets.

Chief fraud advisor (or compliance officer). This person will oversee the work of the investigators and present their reports to the fraud panel. The chief fraud advisor is also responsible for quality control over the work of the investigators and technicalities such as contacting the organization's insurance carrier.

Investigators. The lead investigator will undertake the bulk of work and may employ a small team to assist with this task. He or she may need to call upon accounting, IT, and technical forensic experts from time to time. The investigators may well be from a firm of external consultants. The police department may also be asked to work with the investigators or simply to provide advice and support, although they will take the case on when there is enough evidence to think about prosecution.

Audit committee. The audit committee will want to know that the organization has responded well to the fact of fraud and is managing the problem according to set standards. The chief internal auditor may need to be kept up to date and may provide advice to the investigators regarding corporate systems and procedures. Also, the auditors tend to have access to all organizational information systems and so could be asked to help as appropriate. Some internal audit outfits actually carry out entire fraud investigations and have a pivotal role in all major fraud work.

Definition of Barriers

One aspect of an investigation is to work out what could go wrong. What are the barriers to an effective investigation in conjunction with the set objectives? For larger frauds, it may be a good idea to set up a secure room with a few tables, chairs, marker board, and flip charts so that the investigation team can start to put the fraud into context and bounce ideas around. One flip chart may list the known facts, including people, sections, systems, and the way the crime was perpetrated. Another flip chart may contain a to-do list of tasks that are outstanding and must be completed at some stage. A marker board may be used to brainstorm ideas for advancing the investigation. Things that could get in the way of an investigation are many and varied but could include

- missing or irretrievable documents
- the absence of any known suspects
- time limits before the investigation goes public
- the non-availability or intimidation of witnesses
- the possible involvement of management in the fraud area
- computerized evidence that could be destroyed
- requests by the police to restrict the scope of the investigation
- the need for privacy in interviews
- noncooperation of key witnesses
- apparent alibis of the suspects
- the danger of claims of entrapment
- claims of duress from suspects
- the possibility that the fraud resulted from innocent mistakes or that management authorized the questionable activities
- the unstable mental state of the suspect

Potential barriers must be considered very carefully. One aspect of this stage of the investigation is to get over the barriers, and if possible, get rid of them entirely. Some barriers are legal in that only certain things are allowed by law.

Strategy

Possibly, the most crucial stage of the investigation is that of setting the strategy. The team of investigators may go back to the flip charts and brainstorm how best to deal with the fraud, but at a minimum, it will want to ensure that

- the fraud itself is properly understood;
- the offense is clearly defined in terms of which local and federal laws have been violated;
- the functioning of the systems and controls breached by the fraud is understood;
- the amount lost is established;
- the area affected by the fraud is isolated;

- the people potentially implicated in the fraud are identified; and
- the witnesses who can contribute to the investigation are defined.

The remainder of the strategy is about preserving and gathering the available evidence required to prove the fraud in a way that makes the evidence admissible. For example, if the police take charge of a case, the rules on law enforcement apply, and the employer's investigators become agents of the police. As such, the investigators will need search warrants for carrying out tasks such as desk searches. The assigned investigators will have to be professionals, as they may be required to testify in court.

Full investigation

After the investigation team has been assigned specific tasks, the full investigation may be started. The techniques described earlier, such as interviewing, forensic examination of documents, and so on, will be used in the investigation proper. The main point to note is the need to set a clear objective for each task and ensure that the right resource is assigned to the right job and that the working papers are beyond reproach. Use a standard form for each task that includes sections for

- task objective
- assigned investigator
- method employed
- results
- conclusions

Paperwork, documents, reports, and the results of any analysis can be attached to the front sheet and precisely cross-referenced. Interview records should be carefully prepared and filed along with any attachments relevant to the case. Particular care should be taken with any consent forms received to allow access to personal records and searches to ensure that they have been provided voluntarily, with no duress or inducements. Most investigations are a mix of creative thinking about what to look for and very basic gathering and documentation procedures that are applied meticulously.

Interim reports

It is important to drive fraud investigations so that there is constant momentum in the right direction. Some investigations can be quite frustrating when many hours of work are required to shift through reams of paper—most totally irrelevant—with the possibility of one or two items being highly significant. Even automated interrogations can be boring, as they may flag hundreds of records that have to be manually extracted and scrutinized in detail. Many fraud investigations are time-bound in that a loss is identified, but the case gets older and older as the work establishes what happened. All ongoing investigations should involve interim reporting on a regular basis when

- the investigation is taking a while to complete and lasts more than one week;
- there has been a major change in direction of the investigation as a result of new leads;
- there is clear evidence from which to prepare charges against the suspect;
- a decision is needed on whether to continue the investigation;
- the fraud panel is meeting and needs an update on work in progress; and
- the police or other external bodies need to know of the progress on a case.

If there is a chief fraud advisor (or compliance officer), it may be a good idea for him or her to get an update on outstanding fraud investigations every week or two. For more significant investigations, regular progress reports may be required, perhaps delivered as oral presentations rather than formal reports. The interim report will cover such items as

- the fraud and how it came about
- work carried out to date
- cost of the investigation to date
- details of known losses
- any special problems and sensitivities
- progress of gathering evidence and whether there are any suspects
- any suspension of employees so far
- any charges that are being considered
- further work required and possible time frames involved
- any items submitted for management decision
- any recommendations for management action

Witness statements

Interviewing was described as an important technique in investigations; in a typical inquiry, many dozens of people may be questioned to ascertain the facts. When this task has been completed, formal witness statements may be obtained; that is, a formal record of the events in the words of the witness that is duly completed, signed, and witnessed.

The format of the record should be such that it can be presented in court for civil or criminal action and can also be used as part of an internal disciplinary case against the employee. If the fraud results in a criminal prosecution, the police may wish to re-interview witnesses and obtain their own statements. If the investigator's version is acceptable, then the statements can go straight to the prosecution team—something of a compliment. Any exhibit referred to in the statements should be attached and clearly cross-referenced to the statement.

Suspect interview

This is a most difficult part of the investigation. It is undertaken when there is sufficient evidence of an alleged offense that has to be presented to the suspect to provide an opportunity to address the evidence. A file of evidence will have been compiled, including documents, statements, analysis, surveillance records, and other material relevant to the inquiry. The suspect may be asked to recount his or her understanding of events, and this will be compared with the known facts. When the investigators are in possession of all key facts, they will probably remind the suspects of their rights and place the evidence before them while seeking an explanation of each incriminating item.

Documentation via a written note or tape is essential; some investigators make a video recording of the interview. If there is an admission of guilt, along with dates, times, names, method, and an indication of intent, the interview may have to be terminated. Any statements should be signed voluntarily and include a written note of the suspect's willingness to cooperate and any explanations for the offense offered by the suspect. It may be best to secure a separate statement for each separate offense. When there are sufficient grounds to bring charges against the suspect, again the interview can be terminated.

The interview process should involve no intimidation or duress; it should simply be an attempt to get to the truth. The suspect has the right to make a formal complaint about the interview, and this complaint will have to be properly responded to. The suspect should be asked at the end whether he or she is satisfied with the opportunities given to provide explanations, and additional details can be included if required. The suspects should be given an opportunity to make a full confession, and if the replies are unsatisfactory, they can be asked to rethink their answers. Scenarios that suggest guilt can be laid out before the suspects, and they can be asked to comment. Questions may also be posed about others who may be implicated in the crime.

Final report

The final report is a formal document that may be considered by many different parties. Legal representatives for both the prosecution and the defense, and even a jury, may view the report. External bodies, such as external audit firms or the government if the company is in receipt of government funds, may also wish to consider the report. Insurance carriers and regulatory bodies may request access to the report of the investigation, and the courts may order access by various parties to the proceedings. The point is that the report should be firmly grounded; it should not only look good but also contain a valid account of the scope, findings, and conclusions from the investigation.

Types of reports. There are different types of reports to fit different circumstances. The investigator needs to ensure that the right kind of report is prepared for the right circumstances. Unlike standard reports, a fraud investigation has certain peculiarities that make it a little different. There may be periods of extreme frenzy followed by periods of calm, collected analysis where the findings are harmonized. A simple model of "6 *As*" shown in Figure 4.1, can be used to reflect the changing stages of an investigation and the various reports required. The type of report is linked to the stage that the investigation has

Level One—Alarm. Alarm bells are rung to tell the executives that something is wrong and there may be an employee fraud at hand. This is done via a brief memo that is presented to senior management or the board. An oral statement will highlight the suspicions and the fact that some quick research must be undertaken. A one-page memo may follow the short presentation of the allegations, as time is the essential ingredient here. Any contact with the press that is necessary should be coordinated by the press office.

Level Two—Assess. This stage seeks to drill down a little deeper and tends to happen after the case has been worked on for a few days. The report again is a short document that tries to identify the scale of the fraud and whether this is a big or less significant investigation. A schedule of known and anticipated losses will be the main feature of the written report.

Level Three—Assist. A careful consideration of ways to stop any more losses should be reported, although this will have to be done fairly quickly. The insurance carriers will not be impressed if an organization becomes aware of a problem and then allows it to accelerate and cause more losses than necessary. This report will talk about any quick controls that should be established, and any action, such as suspending a suspect that may be required to halt the fraud. Protection of the organization is the main thrust of this type of report.

Level Four—Alert. This is the longer, more comprehensive stage of the investigation, detailing anyone who is implicated in the offense. The report is longer because of the risk of defamation; the facts will have to be carefully checked and presented before it can be released at all. A formal interim report should link the findings to the detailed evidence with an index and chronological notations. This document may be considered by third parties and may form the basis for decisions regarding charges and police involvement, if this has not yet happened. A draft will go to legal counsel for due consideration before the report is released. Legal admissibility drives the style of this type of report.

Level Five—Advise. A report should eventually be issued that gives clear direction on the appropriateness of criminal prosecution and internal disciplinary action. This report will discuss the offenses committed, the charges that should result, and the determination of how the disciplinary code has been breached. It is hard to think of an employee fraud that does not breach the code of conduct set by most organizations. The fraud panel and audit committee will probably want to see a copy of this report. Problem solving and closure should be key considerations for this report.

Level Six—Assure. This type of report will be a less punchy document that looks at the longer-term implications of fraud risk that has not been properly managed. Aspects of control failure will be examined along with the need to install better controls. The report may stimulate a consultation process whereby buzz groups consider the proposals after formal presentations on any proposed changes to control structures. This report is about achieving assurances that effective controls are in place to guard against the risk of fraud.

Contents. The final report of the investigation should contain all the information needed to understand the various stages of the investigation and will cover matters that are of importance to the recipients. These will obviously vary, but the following areas may be covered:

- The objectives of the investigation
- The scope of the work
- Details of the team carrying out the investigation
- The way the fraud was uncovered
- Details of the fraud itself
- Control weaknesses that meant the fraud was not prevented
- The investigation strategy, reporting lines, and approval procedures involved
- Personal data relating to the suspects (this may be held in a separate confidential appendix). Suspects may be referred to by a code name that should be read in conjunction with the classified personal data in a detachable appendix
- Legal representatives
- Any police involvement
- Offenses committed and possible charges
- Any recovery action that has been initiated
- Detailed list of evidence and conclusions drawn from each item
- Recommendations for supporting criminal prosecution, disciplinary action, and improving controls
- Any other relevant information

A great deal may end up in the official report of the investigation, and terms such as *the suspect* and *alleged offense* should be used to retain objectivity. It is not the job of the report to assess the guilt or innocence of the suspect; that is the job of the courts. The job of the report is simply to document the preceding items clearly and objectively.

Structure. The fraud report should follow a basic structure that makes for easy reading and understanding. It may include, for example:

- *Cover.* This should be marked *Confidential,* and for more sensitive investigations may be coded rather than given a title. It certainly should not display the name of the chief suspect.
- *Executive summary.* Introduction, brief account of the fraud, terms of reference for the investigation, suspects, and proposed charges and recommended actions required.
- *Introduction.* Objectives and scope of the investigation, how the fraud came to be noticed, who was assigned to undertake the work, and their approach.
- *Detailed findings.* Details of the fraud, the offenses resulting from the fraud, description of evidence relating to each offense (in chronological order), and any rebuttals of the evidence.
- *Appendices.* List and summaries of evidence, including witness statements, points by legal advisors, and any other relevant schedules. It is generally best to get the report structure established before drafting the content. Once the structure makes sense, the detail should fit in quite easily.

Action

Reports should be action-oriented. That is, they should lead to efficient action to deal with the problems that have been identified and encourage a response to any recommendations made by the investigating team. The problem is that a report alone does not necessarily lead to direct action; hence, this is a separate stage of the investigation. The reporting process should be fine-tuned so that the right people have access to the report and are able to make executive decisions. This is a fundamental point in that investigators work on behalf of the employing organization and provide specialist advice based on the work carried out.

It really is the organization, in the guise of the board and CEO, that needs to take responsibility for acting on the results of the investigation. Missing funds should be traced through lawyers who specialize in tracking and freezing relevant funds with a view to recovery. Illegal funds may be transferred to family members by a fraudster or laundered into investments and schemes that fall outside the purview of the investigators, and may even be transferred abroad.

Note that the Office of International Trade may provide assistance in tracing missing funds. The organization will also need to consider whether any case against the alleged fraudster is likely to be successful and weigh the amounts involved and the costs of taking civil action for recovery. Likewise, the case for seeking a criminal prosecution will also have to be examined.

Review

The final stage of the investigation is often missed completely. This stage entails a reflective consideration of what went wrong and why. The review may cover a variety of areas, including, for example:

- How did the fraud happen, and why was it allowed to continue for the period in question?
- What controls have failed and how do we correct the problem?
- What about the overall control environment and culture in place—should they be changed?
- How is our staff managing the risk of fraud?
- Could a similar fraud happen in another part of the organization?
- Did we do enough to recover lost funds?
- Are our procedures for carrying out fraud investigations adequate?
- How did we handle potential damage to our corporate reputation?
- What are the main lessons we can take away from this experience?

Reflection Menu

1. The evidence obtained during an investigation may be directly derived from the fraud, or it may be circumstantial and include
   a. Witness statements, circumstantial evidence, financial reports on the suspect, physical evidence, documentary evidence, demonstrative evidence, and analytical data
   b. Witness statements, circumstantial evidence, financial reports on the suspect, physical and social evidence, documentary evidence, demonstrative evidence, and analytical data
   c. Witness evidence, circumstantial evidence, financial reports on the suspect, physical and social evidence, documentary evidence, demonstrative evidence, and analytical data
   d. Witness evidence, circumstantial evidence, financial reports on the suspect, physical evidence, documentary evidence, demonstrative evidence, and analytical data

2. Investigative techniques include the following EXCEPT
   a. observing rights and maintaining staff morale, evidence, interviewing
   b. observing rights and maintaining staff morale, nonverbal communication
   c. observing rights and maintaining staff morale, analytical review, surveillance
   d. observing rights and maintaining staff morale, examination of auditing

3. Most communication between two people occurs nonverbally which may include
   a. spatial factors, body language, facial expressions, silences, voice and language
   b. Spatial factors, body language, facial expressions, silences, voice and looking

c. Spatial factors, body language, facial expressions, signs, voice and language
d. Spatial factors, body language, facial expressions, silences, speech and language

(For the answers, please turn to Appendix A.)

5 Money Laundering

Introduction

The Financial Action Task Force (FATF) is an intergovernmental body whose purpose is the development and promotion of policies to combat money laundering and terrorist financing. It is the body that sets and monitors international standards for anti–money laundering regulations. The FATF has defined "money laundering" as the processing of criminal proceeds to disguise their illegal origin in order to legitimize the ill-gotten gains of crime.

Money laundering is a process that aims to disguise the existence, nature, source, control, beneficial ownership, location, and disposition of property derived from criminal activity. In this context, property assumes the wider definition of that which is physical, intangible, or represented in the form of rights or obligations such as a pension funds or trust fund.

The Money Laundering Process

The objective of tax fraudsters and of those involved in a wide range of criminal activities is to disguise the source of money and to convert the "dirty money" and "wash it" into a form that will be difficult to retrace its origins such as placing the "dirty money" in bank accounts, real estate, stocks, insurance premiums and other assets, which can be used later without raising suspicion. Whether the crime is a tax crime or is related to trafficking in narcotics, illegal sales of weapons, corruption, or any of a vast range of criminal activities, the basic process that money launderers use to turn illicit proceeds into apparently legal monies or assets is globally accepted as having three stages— placement, layering, and integration. These are the three phases of money laundering often referred to as the money-laundering triad. The integration phase may be further divided into two sub-phases—justification and investment.

Placement

This initial stage is considered by many as the riskiest part for criminals to achieve as they attempt to introduce the proceeds of a crime into the financial system. The goal in this stage is to deposit criminal proceeds, generally cash, into a bank account at home or abroad. Although banks have been used for facilitating this stage in the past—for example, by narcotics traffickers' making cash deposits at local branches—the banks' AML systems and controls have become and are perceived to be increasingly sophisticated, and launderers have sought alternative means of placing their illicit cash.

For this purpose, cash could be switched into other valuables like trade goods, diamonds, gold bars or cheques. It could also be exchanged into other currencies in larger denominations and/or split up in smaller sums, which allow easy transportation by cash couriers. Another method is to infiltrate cash-intensive businesses—such as restaurants and other public venues—to provide a plausible explanation for the movement of large amounts of cash. Recent proposals to regulate casinos and other gambling businesses, for example, respond to a perceived vulnerability to money laundering. When this scheme succeeds, "dirty" money is coming led with income derived from the legitimate business and deposited with a bank.

The cash or other valuables can be transported abroad, away from the country where the crime was committed, to the country of residence of the criminal or a specific country where cash can be easily deposited or invested. Transportation can be by car, plane (passengers or cargo), or by using an underground banking system. For all of these acts, criminals can use third parties, either individuals or corporations. Financial fraud, by contrast, may not necessarily have a placement stage in the conventional sense. The funds may already be in the financial system, particularly when a financial institution has been defrauded.

Money derived from fraud, like tax fraud or investment fraud, could easily be money held in a bank account and capable of being exchanged electronically. Not all criminal proceeds are in the form of cash or even money. Goods from theft can be exchanged for other valuables.

Layering

Once the cash has been successfully placed in the financial system, the launderer typically initiates a number of related transactions with a view to obscuring the origin of the funds by undermining any trace of an audit trail. The goal in this stage is the concealment of the criminal origin of the proceeds. Therefore, money can be transferred and split frequently between bank accounts, countries, individuals and/or corporations, or move the funds between financial products between institutions and between jurisdictions. Money can also be withdrawn in cash and deposited into bank accounts with other banks. It is common to use bank accounts in countries with strict banking secrecy laws and to nominate offshore corporations as the bank account holders.

Integration

Finally, the laundered funds need to be extracted from the financial system so that they can be used to acquire legitimate assets or finance further criminal activities. At that point, the funds or assets have a veneer of respectability within the legitimate economy. The integration phase may be further divided into two sub-phases—justification and investment.

Integration: Justification

The goal in this stage is to create an apparent legal origin for the criminal proceeds. This can be done by

- doing business with yourself (falsifying sources of income, capital gains, and/or loans);
- disguising the ownership of assets; and
- Using criminal proceeds in transactions with third parties.

The money launderer creates an apparent legal origin of the money by fabricating transactions (invoices, bookkeeping, and agreements), with the use of false and fabricated documents such as invoices, reports, contracts, agreements, deeds, as well as written or spoken statements. Common justification methods used are:

- Fabricating a loan—loan-back or back to back;
- Fabricating a rise in net worth—buying and selling real estate and other items,
- Fabricating casino winnings, lottery prizes, inheritance, etc.;
- Disguising the ownership of assets and interest in businesses (constructions with foreign legal entities, e.g. offshore companies or relatives as legal owner);
- Price-manipulating (over- and under-invoicing);
- Manipulating turnover/sales by commingling illicit and legal sources of income.

Integration: Investment

The goal in this final stage is to use criminal proceeds for personal benefit. Cash or electronic money can be used for:

○ Safekeeping—cash on hand;
○ Consumption—day-to-day expenditures, lifestyle, jewellery, vehicles, yachts, art;
○ Investing—bank accounts, real estate, stocks, securities, receivables, funding of legal and illegal business activities.

Criminals may want to display their wealth and wealthy lifestyle by acquiring "badges of wealth" such as luxury homes, vehicles, boats, jewellery, etc. Criminals will seek to launder the proceeds from their crimes to pay for these in order to avoid detection by the tax or law enforcement authorities.

Money Laundering Business

Using a Legitimate Business to Launder Funds

One of the most common methods of laundering funds is to filter the money through a legitimate business (also known as a "front" business). A front business can be a very effective way to launder money because it provides a safe place for organising and managing criminal activity. A front doing legitimate business provides cover for delivery and transportation related to illegal activity. In addition, such a business provides an unsuspicious venue for the comings and goings of large numbers of people. Expenses from illegal activity can be attributed to the legitimate enterprise, and the illegal revenues can be easily placed into the enterprise.

Three methods most commonly used to hide assets or launder money through a front business are:

Overstatement of Reported Revenues

Overstating revenues, also known as *income statement laundering*, occurs when the money launderer records more income on the books of a business than is actually generated by that business. The fictitious revenue accounts for the illegal funds that are secretly inserted into the company.

Overstatement of Reported Expenses

The disadvantage of overstating revenues is that taxes will be due on the income reported. Therefore, if a company overstates its revenue, it will also want to overstate its expenses to offset its tax liability. The fictitious expenses also enable the perpetrator to siphon money back out of the business in order to make payoffs, buy illegal goods, or invest in other criminal ventures. Overstating expenses can be accomplished very easily by reporting payments for supplies never received, professional services never rendered, or wages for fictitious employees.

Balance Sheet Laundering

Rather than attempting to disguise money as normal business revenue, excess funds can simply be deposited into the bank account of the business. This technique is known as balance sheet laundering because it is independent of the money that flows in and out of the business.

Favourite Businesses for Hiding or Laundering Money

In general terms, the businesses chosen for money laundering possess one or more of the following characteristics:

- *Revenue.* A revenue base is difficult to measure because most revenue comes from cash transactions with a highly variable amount per customer. This allows extra money to be brought into the business and disguised as revenue.

- *Expense.* Expenses that are variable and difficult to measure can enable the launderer to extract money from the front business without giving rise to undue suspicion.
- *History.* Historical ties are generally with the ethnic base of a particular criminal group or with industries that have traditionally served as a base for criminal activity.

a. Bars, restaurants, and nightclubs

Businesses that are commonly used to front money laundering operations include bars, restaurants, and nightclubs. These businesses charge relatively high prices, and customers vary widely in their purchases. Sales are generally in cash, and it is notoriously difficult to match the cost of providing food, liquor, and entertainment with the revenues they produce. Fast-food restaurants are also frequently used to front for money laundering operations. Although they tend to charge lower prices than other types of restaurants, most of their sales are made in cash, and expenses can be easily inflated.

b. Vending machines

Vending machine operations also possess many characteristics favourable to a money laundering operation. They have a highly variable and difficult to measure volume of cash receipts, and in large operations, there is a fair amount of flexibility with various transportation, installation, and promotion expenses, providing cover for the withdrawal of laundered funds.

c. Wholesale distribution

Wholesale distribution businesses have historically been a prominent part of money laundering. The revenues in a wholesaling business are not typically as flexible as in food service and vending machine operations, but with a diverse product line and falsified invoices, it is still possible to inject a good deal of illegal cash into the business. More importantly, the industry is ideal for money laundering from the standpoint of expenses. The activities required to run this kind of business are so diverse and difficult to measure that expenses are easy to inflate. Furthermore, a wholesale business' buildings, warehouses, transportation fleet, and its contact with retail establishments are all attractive factors. Many of the classic criminal activities (drugs, fencing, and contraband) are themselves nothing more than distribution operations and can hide behind this type of business cover.

d. Real estate purchases

Real estate purchases are also attractive because (at least historically) real estate increases in value. In addition, rental income can be altered on the books to launder more funds.

e. ATMs

Law enforcement officials are also reporting an increasing use of automatic teller machines (ATMs) to launder money. ATMs can be purchased for as little as US$3,000. Money launderers purchase the machines and place them either in establishments they control or in legitimate businesses. The machines work the same as any other ATM machine, and all transactions are legitimate. The money launderer simply fills the machine with cash from illegal activities. The customer uses the machine and never realises the source of the cash. The ATM banking system debits the cardholders account and credits the ATM owner's bank account. At the end of the month, the launderer receives a bank statement showing funds being deposited from a legitimate financial institution. This option is attractive for money launderers because there are currently no regulations governing the use and operation of privately-owned ATMS. There is no requirement to check the backgrounds of purchasers of the machines, and there are no mandatory reporting procedures and no rules for maintaining ATM sales records.

f. Calling in a specialist
    Converting ill-gotten gains into cashier's cheques or money orders is not particularly difficult for even the most unsophisticated criminal. However, because many launderers fear detection, they turn to more sophisticated specialists. *Couriers* arrange for the transportation of money to a site where it is converted into another form of currency. For instance, drug traffickers will physically transport money to a foreign jurisdiction where it is deposited into a bank account or converted directly to cheques or money orders. Since the courier has no apparent connection with the true owner of the funds, the money launderer retains his anonymity.

White-collar professionals such as attorneys, accountants, and brokers, might also serve to launder illegal funds. Through investments, trust accounts, fund transfers, and tax avoidance schemes, these professionals can manipulate the financial, commercial, and legal systems to conceal the origin and ownership of assets.

Why Do Money Launderers Launder?

Money launderers could be classified into four categories:

A. Those who commit predicate offenses and launder their own money;
B. Those who commit predicate offenses, launder their own money, and also launder the proceeds of other criminals;

C. Those in business who do not commit predicate offenses but launder the proceeds of others' crimes as part of their otherwise legitimate business;

D. Those who launder the proceeds of others' crimes as their only business activity.

Category A. Those in category A (above)—individuals who *commit predicate offenses and launder their own money*—do so out of necessity. Their successful predicate acquisitive crimes generate money, and anything they then do with that money is criminalized as money laundering. The only way they can stop laundering is to stop their predicate criminal activity. It is interesting to think that the vast majority of all of those who commit money laundering are not doing so by choice.

That necessity suggests that they will not be, indeed cannot be, deterred by AML measures alone. And yet, that is what anti–money launderers limit themselves to in their thinking and in their actions. In order to influence the choices and behaviors of category A laun-derers, the anti–money launderers need to focus on undermining the motive for the predicate offence, not just the laundering activity. We can achieve that in part by creating a strong likelihood that every acquisition crime will fail by being detected and end in the total and permanent confiscation of all gains. We must therefore assess whether the global AML efforts are affecting the minds and behav-iors of this category of money launderer to the extent that they are turning away from a life of predicate crime. There is little or no study demonstrating the extent to which the confiscation of one criminal's accrued proceeds demotivates other criminals to the extent that they turn toward a law-abiding life. Such a deterrent effect should be at the core of our AML efforts, particularly deterring the young and potential next generation of acquisitive criminals, and yet, nothing in our international standards, national legislations, or regulations drives targeted influencing activity nor measurement of sociological effect.

Financial Action Task Force (FATF) is reviewing and revising the international mutual evaluation standards with more attention on effectiveness. This should result in some improvements, but international thinking is not sufficiently ambitious to consider such strategic social effects. One can imagine that if the sons of criminals were to witness the undoing of their fathers, the loss of everything the family has become accustomed to after many years of a lavish lifestyle and the inevitable stresses and breakups of family relationships, they might draw the conclusion that crime really isn't worth it in the end. These youngsters, the potential next criminal generation, might then go on to choose another life path, both law abiding and socially acceptable.

Unfortunately, the affected criminal himself does not react in such a way. We can draw on the findings of psychologist Burrhus Frederic Skinner to assert that the offender does not associate punishment with the crime when it follows too long afterward (confiscation is often many years after the crime), but rather believes the punisher to be unjust. This is further reason for the anti–money launderers to do all they can to shorten the time lapse between offense and confiscation.

Category B. The minds and behaviours of those in category B— those who *commit predicate offenses, launder their own money, and also launder the proceeds of other criminals.* They are, in essence, similar creatures to category A, but additionally, they choose to launder the proceeds of the crimes of others. This behavior is not driven by necessity like our previous group nor by greed; it is driven by the need to be loved. Abraham Maslow's *Hierarchy of Needs* identified the human needs for love, acceptance, and belonging as drivers for behavior, followed by the need for self-esteem and the esteem of others.

These launderers are increasing their criminal social status by assisting others; they want to be admired, respected, and even needed. Their sense of self-worth increases in proportion to their circle of reliant associates. This desire to be loved is a vulnerability that can be exploited by the anti–money launderers. The respect from criminal peers needs to be overwhelmed by societal odium; we should shape a society in which the risk of being unloved by many is greater than the likelihood of being loved by a few. However, globally there is little or no public disdain attached to money laundering. Some jurisdictions have run campaigns to raise public awareness, and while many of these have resulted in spikes of public reporting, there is no enduring social stigma. Other jurisdictions have attempted to name and shame convicted offenders (though rarely money launderers), but in my personal view, these campaigns tend to miss the most crucial issue. The offenders and their criminal peers perceive the shame to lie in getting caught, not in committing the crime, and there is sometimes latent respect amongst the public for criminal audacity (for example, there is often a positive, almost romantic, status attributed to jewel thieves and bank robbers by the public.)

Shaming for AML offenses needs to methodically influence by building fact-based beliefs concerning the range of real life harms caused to individuals, businesses, communities, and societies. By increasing emotional responses against laundering activities, and by presenting concrete recommendations for action, we stand a far greater chance of influencing activity.

Currently, there is nothing in our international standards, national legislations, or regulations to drive targeted influencing activity in this area or measurement of public opinion.

Category C. The third category (C) covers *those people in businesses who do not commit predicate offenses but launder the proceeds of others' crimes as part of their otherwise legitimate business.* These money launderers can be found across nearly all industries, not only in the regulated financial sectors. These are individuals or groups of individuals who own, or are employed in, legitimate businesses and who choose to accept monies that they know or reasonably suspect to be derived from crime. Those who neither know nor suspect are excluded; these people are victims rather than conspirators. And also those who accept and launder the money are excluded but do so within the laws of the land by reporting their activities to the relevant authorities, for example. Readers from the business sector should realize that this third category includes fellow employees. In order to understand why an otherwise law-abiding employee should choose to launder criminal proceeds, we can look again at Maslow's *Hierarchy of Needs*.

One of the basic needs is security; for example, the trigger could be a failing business, the threat of unemployment, or even a physical threat. Provided these reasons are genuine, then any person in this category is a victim (of circumstance) and needs to be protected. In the wider world, there are many effective strategies to prevent people from falling victim to a range of temptation and threat, but once again, there is little or nothing in our international standards, national legislations, or regulations to protect persons/businesses and prevent money laundering. It is, perhaps, more startling still that there is no way to measure the preventative effect.

Category D. The fourth category (D) represents career criminals—those who *launder the proceeds of others' crimes as their only business activity.* For these people, their lifestyle choice is to launder the proceeds of/from the crimes of others. They are either former acquisitive crime group members who change their roles and risk exposure from a perceived "*hard edge*" crime to a more sophisticated "*white-collar*" and often ambiguous area of crime, or they are a category C person who has benefited from high commissions, enjoyed the attraction of being associated with (and loved by) the underworld, and who has either not received any overt attention from the anti–money launderers (including previous employers), or who has successfully seen them off.

They are driven by necessity—it is their livelihood—by the need to belong and be needed, to be respected as a professional, and ultimately to realize their own potential or "*self-actualization,*" a state reached by a minority of the population. Such a range of needs presents an open field of vulnerabilities for the creative and free-thinking anti–money launderers.

AML and Forensic Accounting Investigation

When money laundering is suspected or controls are considered vulnerable to abuse, a forensic accounting investigator with the requisite knowledge of AML may be engaged to undertake an investigation, a compliance diagnostic, or a controls review. In general, a money-laundering investigation usually begins with the detail rather than with high-level controls and reviews transactions and documentation related to specific customers.

From such a process, the forensic accounting investigator charged with executing the review generally will form a bottom-up view of the controls environment and ascertain whether it complies with the regulatory regime governing that jurisdiction. Although the scope of AML assignments is determined on a case-by-case basis, in practice, all three aspects—investigation (including background checks and interviews), compliance diagnostic, and controls review—are likely to be reflected to varying degrees.

The assignments themselves are likely to come from one of two sources at the request of the regulator or of the institution. These assignments are distinctly different from financial statement audits in that they focus specifically on compliance with relevant laws and regulations as well as on particular suspicious transactions and not on financial accounting processes or the entity's reported financial results.

At the request of the regulator

The regulator may seek the involvement of a forensic accounting investigator for a variety of reasons: the regulator could suspect that the institution has perpetrated financial crime or been the victim of financial crime and accordingly authorizes an investigation. Alternatively, the regulator could request an AML review before it is willing to grant a financial license or authorization. The regulator could also request a review as part of a wider but more routine examination of an institution's systems and controls.

Law enforcement officials may also investigate whether an institution was aiding and abetting money laundering through systemic deficiencies or major control failures that permitted the money-laundering activity to remain undetected. Faced with a challenge of that kind, the institution may wish to engage forensic accountants with specialized AML knowledge.

At the request of the institution

Of its own volition, the institution could engage a forensic accounting investigator to undertake a money-laundering-investigation assignment. One of the more common instances is a review in advance of a regulatory visit to identify areas that may need to be addressed. However, the institution may also require a money-laundering review as part of a wider strategic-vulnerability assessment.

A review also may be appropriate in conjunction with an acquisition. The assignment could involve a review of the target's systems and controls or an assessment of the risk profile of its customer base to determine whether any pricing adjustments to the proposed deal might be appropriate.

In the course of an AML review, a forensic accounting investigator should consider all five of the areas that make up the typical AML system and controls, ranging from policies and procedures and customer due diligence to monitoring and reporting, training, and record keeping. All of these areas enter into a thorough AML review, starting with a detailed examination of transactions and records and concluding with an assessment of the overall corporate culture.

Potential Red Flags

The accounting and auditing profession and its authoritative organizations and regulators around the world increasingly recognize the importance and value of AML training and awareness for practitioners in a wide variety of business roles. Internal and external auditors, forensic accounting investigators, managerial accountants, compliance officers, attorneys, business executives, and board members may find it useful to be mindful of the following potential red flags, which may indicate that the entity in question is being used for purposes other than those stated in its public documents.

The following transactions may indicate money laundering is taking place. The list should be used to identify those transactions and customers that may require further investigation.

- Large purchase of a lump sum contract where the customer typically purchases small, regular payment contracts
- Use of a third-party cheque to make a purchase or investment
  - Lack of concern for the performance of an investment but great concern for the early cancellation of the contract
- Use of cash as payment for a transaction, which is typically handled by cheques or other forms of payment
  - Makes lump sum payments by wire transfer or with foreign currency
- Reluctance to provide normal information when setting up a policy or account or providing minimal information
- Purchase of investments in amounts considered beyond the customer's apparent means
- Use of a letter of credit or other methods of trade finance to move money between countries where such trade is inconsistent with customer's usual pattern
- Establishment of a large investment policy and within a short time period, customer requests cancellation of the policy, and cash value paid to third party
- Use of wire transfers to move large amounts of money to or from a financial haven country such as the Cayman Islands, Colombia, Hong Kong, Liechtenstein, Luxembourg, Panama, or Switzerland
- Request to borrow maximum cash value of single premium policy soon after paying for policy
- Unusual cash transactions
- Payment to or receipts from jurisdictions regarded as high risk (listed under the FATF's NCCT initiative)
- Frequent deposits or withdrawals just below reporting thresholds

A trend in the development of AML regimes around the world is to expand beyond the banking sector and incorporate other types of business, including professional services firms, within the scope of regulation. If accounting and law firms, for example, were to be included within the AML regime, they would be likely to encounter some of the following:

- Specific policies and procedures addressing the money-laundering risks in their business and measures introduced to mitigate those risks
- Client identification procedures, including documentary standards and requirements
- Internal and external reporting arrangements to facilitate the reporting of any suspicious activity identified in the course of auditing a client
- Training to ensure that staff are aware of their individual responsibilities and have the necessary tools to discharge those responsibilities
- Record keeping, including length of time that client identification needs to be retained and the degree to which it needs to be accessible.

Money Laundering Indicators for Individuals

When performing the audit or examining the tax return, there are factors to consider that will assist in identifying possible cases of money laundering. These factors or "indicators" may require simple observation skills as well as the examination of the taxpayer's documentation. When individuals spend their criminal proceeds on the acquisition or use of assets and do not have enough legitimate income to explain their expenditures, this is regarded as "unusual use" or "unusual possession" of assets. This in turn raises suspicion. Some criminals will attempt to conceal the origin of the funds by creating an apparently legitimate origin. Pretending that the origin of the funds is legitimate can be done by using criminal money to carry out business transactions with oneself or with third parties.

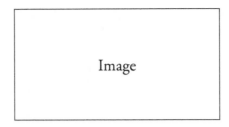

Examples: *Taxpayer appears to be living beyond their means*

A low family income usually indicates that there are limited opportunities for buying, owning, or consuming expensive assets. Perhaps the expensive items were bought with additional income from crime. The following are examples of such discrepancies:

1. A shareholder's financial contributions to a business are not in line with the individual's tax returns;
2. There is an accumulation of personal wealth when the only known source of funds is from a business source that cannot support it;
3. An examination of personal bank records does not show funds available to support the lifestyle;
4. A taxpayer uses offshore credit/debit cards, and the source of funds to support the account cannot be identified.

Combating Money Laundering

Criminals accumulate significant sums of money by committing crimes such as drug trafficking, human trafficking, theft, investment fraud, extortion, corruption, embezzlement, and tax fraud. Money laundering is a serious threat to the legal economy and affects the integrity of financial institutions. It also changes the economic power in certain sectors. If left unchecked, it will corrupt society as a whole. Fighting money laundering serves several purposes.

i. *The social importance*

Crime causes tangible and intangible damage to third parties, individuals, and society as a whole. Money laundering can result in reducing the public's confidence in certain professions such as lawyers, accountants, and notaries and economic sectors such as real estate, hospitality and banks, and other financial institutions. Investing the proceeds of crime may also distort competition between businesses and entrepreneurs. Money laundering allows the criminal to start, continue, and expand activities in legitimate sectors of the economy. It may create a perception that crime pays and may also have a stimulating effect on our youth starting a criminal career.

ii. *To identify tax crimes*

Unusual transactions can be an indication of tax crimes in the past and can lead to the identification of those involved.

iii. *To identify other crimes and criminals*

Taxing the income of criminals according to tax rules alone will not lead to the identification of potential money laundering. It will not stop crime from happening or from being profitable. The detection of unusual transactions may assist in identifying criminals and their illegal activities. Sharing information with law enforcement authorities can lead to the start of a criminal investigation.

iv. *To locate and confiscate criminal assets*

Identifying unusual transactions can provide insight into the flow of money and the destination of laundered criminal proceeds into assets such as real estate, vehicles, yachts, and bank accounts. This will assist law enforcement authorities in seizing those assets during a criminal investigation.

Enforcement and Prevention Strategies

Financial institutions, brokers, and insurance companies should be aware and should make their employees aware of situations that could indicate money laundering activity.

a. Policy Statement

All entities covered under the reporting and record-keeping laws and regulations should have a written policy against handling the proceeds of drug trafficking or other criminal activity. The statement should provide that the institution requires its employees to operate with the highest moral and ethical principles. It should include refusing to do business with criminals and money launderers; a commitment to conduct business only with legitimate business organizations; refusing to do business with businesses that refuse to provide proper documentation of their identity and purpose; referring all suspicious transactions to the appropriate department who will then decide whether to refer the case to law enforcement; and a commitment to comply with the spirit of and the specific provisions of the law.

b. "Know Your Customer" Programs

Many financial institutions have "Know Your Customer" programs. Such programs should provide for effective customer identification, account monitoring, and appropriate action in suspicious circumstances.

c. New Deposit Accounts

For individual deposit accounts, minimum identification standards should be established. The information to be obtained should include:
   o Name • Address • Date of birth • Government-issued ID number

- Current employer • Business and residence telephone numbers

The person should be required to submit some form of identification that includes a photo such as a driver's licence or passport, and a copy should be made and kept in the customer's file. If there are any doubts or inconsistencies about the information provided, the employee should be instructed to notify the appropriate department.

Minimum standards for new business accounts should include:

- Business name and address
- Telephone number
- Taxpayer identification number
- Documents establishing the formation of the business entity (articles of incorporation, partnership agreement, etc.)
- Copies of all assumed name filings or DBAs (doing business as)
- A full description of the operations of the business
- Credit and banking references
- The identity of the officers, directors, or other principals.

The account representative should also consider making a personal visit to the customer's place of business. Besides promoting good customer relations, a personal visit will help identify whether the business is legitimate or simply a front. The representative can also use this opportunity to get to know the principals of the business.

An institution should perform due diligence in establishing a new loan account because if the customer is engaged in money laundering, there is a risk of forfeiture of collateral pledged on the loans. Real or personal property that is traceable to drug sales or that is purchased with laundered funds is subject to seizure by the government. If the property seized is pledged as collateral, the financial institution must prove that it was an innocent lien holder of the property who had no knowledge of the illegal activity. Minimum standards regarding the information to be gathered should include:

- Reliable identifying information similar to that required for new deposit accounts
- Reliable financial information such as financial statements and copies of tax returns
- The purpose of the loan
- Credit history and prior banking references
- Verifiable, legitimate means of repayment
- Assurance that the loan amount is consistent with the purpose of the loan and the nature of the business

d. Services for Non-Accountholders

Banks often issue cashier's cheques, money orders, traveller's cheques and perform currency exchanges, wire transfers, or cheque cashing services. Strict identification requirements should be established for transactions with persons who are not regular bank customers. In fact, regulations require that in some instances banks keep a record of the identity of persons who are not established customers. Such regulations usually require at a minimum the person's name and address, driver's licence number (or other number of identifying document produced), and social insurance number or employer identification number.

e. Monitoring Accounts

While identification of customers is important, it is equally important to monitor the activity of accounts. The institution should identify unusual transactions that might not be consistent with the normal business of the customer. Unusual and dramatic changes in wire transfer, monetary instrument, and cheque transactions are important to identify. If unusual transactions or activities are noted, the institution should take some action to protect itself.

The appropriate action in some cases might be to discuss the changes with the customer to find out the reasons therefore. Increased transactions might be the result of an increase in sales or the result of a promotional activity. However, if the discussion leads to a reasonable suspicion that the transactions are illegitimate, the institution might be required to notify the appropriate government agency.

Detection

- *Incoming and outgoing wire transfer logs* can help companies identify possible patterns suggestive of money laundering.
- *Account activity reports* generally show weekly or monthly balances, deposits, and withdrawals. Review of these statements can identify those accounts with large increases in average balances and numbers of transactions.
- *Policy cancellation reports* should identify policies cancelled within a specific time period. Report details should include the amount of the cash surrender value, the identity of the sales agent, and the actual term of the policy.

Program for AML-Regulated Businesses

a. Written Compliance Program

Businesses should have a regulator-approved AML policy framework, enterprise-wide guidance and standards, implementation policies, and robust operating procedures that integrate compliance into the business and into support areas of consequence. The written AML compliance program should clearly articulate mechanisms for discharging business unit and individual AML responsibilities.

The institution is also expected to consider appropriate controls to authorize policy and procedural variances. Increasingly, there is an expectation that the institution should carry out and document its own risk assessment— that is, its own assessment of the vulnerability of its products and services to money laundering and the corresponding controls that have been introduced to mitigate these risks.

Institutions are also expected to transform risk assessment into a continuous and sustainable process.

b. Minimum Standards of Customer Due Diligence

The AML requirements also stipulate the circumstances in which customers or counterparties need to be identified and the extent to which identity needs to be verified and documentation reviewed. The documentary requirements should vary according to the type of customer—for example, the requirements for an offshore trust are tougher than those for a private individual—and the extent to which the immediate customer is acting on behalf of another. In addition, KYC principles have come to apply to employees, vendors, agents, and other external service providers.

c. Activity Monitoring and Reporting

After accepting a customer or counterparty and opening an account, the institution is likely to have an obligation to monitor customer activity for evidence of money laundering and, depending on the AML regime, other reportable suspicious conditions. When money laundering is identified or suspected, a report should be made to an appropriate external authority. In many jurisdictions, the relevant external authority is the nominated Financial Intelligence Unit (FIU).

There are now more than fifty national FIUs globally, and most of them are members of the international FIU union, the Egmont Group. Although there is a common requirement to report to a nominated authority, the specific role of the FIU varies depending on a number of factors, which are in turn functions of the technical and legal framework established for the unit and the FIU infrastructure. The larger, better-funded FIUs include the Financial Crimes Enforcement Network (FinCEN) of the United States, the United Kingdom's National Criminal Intelligence Unit (NCIS), France's Traitement du renseignement et action contre les circuits financiers clandestins (Tracfin), Canada's

Financial Transactions Reports Analysis Centre (FinTrac), and Australia's Australian Transactions and Reports Analysis Centre (AUSTRAC) that has been created.

While some FIUs may simply collate and analyze information received and then forward it to another authority for investigation, others play a more active regulatory role in the administration of the country's AML regime. The FIU is often responsible for undertaking compliance examinations, issuing fines and penalties, providing disclosure information, and drafting regulations. The US Financial Crimes Enforcement Network (FinCEN) is both anAML policy-making and enforcement agency.

d. Training

As well as documenting its approach to AML in its policies and procedures, the institution should ensure that AML policies and procedures are communicated to staff via training on a regular basis. Training is likely to cover obligations under the law circumstances that could indicate that products and services are being used for money-laundering purposes, and when and to whom suspicions should be reported. AML training needs to be tailored to the needs and circumstances of the trainees and to be continually refreshed and tracked.

e. Record Keeping

Finally, the institution should consider storage and retention policies for AML related documents. The documents should include evidence obtained when verifying customer identity, suspicious transaction reports made internally, reports submitted externally to the FIU, and records of training. In certain jurisdictions, AML obligations go even further. In Germany and Switzerland, for example, auditors have an obligation to monitor and report on a bank's compliance with AML legislation and regulation. In the US, the obligation lies primarily with the business.

Within the regulated sector, customers, products and services, channels, and service providers have their own profiles of AML risk. Banking relationships, for example, are likely to be higher risk because they facilitate regular receipts and payments to third parties without the verification of the third party. That risk is magnified when wire transfers are available because funds can then be moved between jurisdictions. At the other end of the risk spectrum are products involving small regular payments that are repayable only to the account holder and products include certain insurance contracts and personal investment plans, among other instruments. Although no institution is immune to money laundering, its AML policies, procedures, systems, and other controls should realistically correspond to the money-laundering risks posed.

The company's regulated status will inform its general attitude toward money laundering, AML, and financial crime. Some financial institutions have appointed directors responsible for financial crime, including fraud and money laundering. In the United States, AML compliance officers are legally required at covered financial institutions.

A company's regulated status and the attitude of the board and senior management—that is, the tone at the top—have impact on the extent and quality of the control environment. At a minimum, AML compliance should respond to regulatory requirements. In more sophisticated organizations, those responsible for AML typically are informing other aspects of the business, such as acquisition strategies, introduction of new products and services, entry into new distribution channels, and development and deployment of new technologies.

Impact of Money Laundering

On Financial Statements

The impact of money laundering on financial statements should be considered in terms of both direct and indirect consequences on fairly representing the state of a business. While the direct impact is clearly important, the indirect consequences can be just as significant, and they are often underestimated by management. Money launderers tend to use the business entity more as a conduit than as a means of directly expropriating assets. For this reason, money laundering is far less likely to affect financial statements than is a fraud such as asset misappropriation.

Consequently, it is unlikely to be detected in a financial statement audit. In addition, other forms of fraudulent activity usually result in the loss or disappearance of assets or revenue, whereas money laundering involves the manipulation of large quantities of illicit proceeds to distance them from their source quickly and without drawing attention. Although money laundering rarely has a direct impact on financial statements, it may also have other consequences of concern. The consequences could be any of the following.

- *Law enforcement interest.* Law enforcement agencies may act on the suspicion that a business has been infiltrated by money launderers. A significant amount of time can be expended responding to requests from law enforcement agencies, ranging from discovery requests and disclosure orders to asset-freeze orders.
- *Regulatory revocation.* A financial services business could have its license and charter revoked in the event that a significant breach in its AML systems and controls is discovered.
- *Operational catastrophe.* There is also the possibility of civil seizure of assets or shareholder derivative suits when it is determined that the institution was negligent in its duties and facilitated the movement of funds.

- *Reputational damage.* Perhaps the most significant implication for an institution is the reputational risk accompanying the incidence or even the allegation of money laundering.

This combination of the respectable and disrespectable, of business and crime, is an attractive proposition for the media. As well, the discovery of money laundering at an institution could undermine the trust of previously loyal savers and investors, prompting them to look elsewhere. A brand in which significant resources have been invested could be harmed if money laundering is alleged or discovered. In sum, although money laundering may not have a direct impact on financial statements, it has the potential to expose a company or financial institution to considerable risk.

On Companies

Both fraud and money laundering may result in criminal activity, but perhaps equally significant to companies and financial institutions is the reputational risk associated with those activities. The media interest in Enron, WorldCom, and other massive frauds in recent years is indicative of the public appetite for stories involving crime and big business. Whenever such a story breaks, it often is difficult for the company under siege to manage the public relations impact. Not only can share prices fall dramatically, as in the Bank of New York money-laundering case in the late 1990s, but also any investment by a company in building its brands may be at risk.

The extent to which a company, its board of directors, and its senior management are focused on money laundering is guided in part by whether or not the company is regulated. The extent to which a company or institution *must* have specific AML systems and controls depends on whether its industry and/or sector is regulated for AML purposes. Today, the degree of regulation varies considerably among AML regimes around the globe. Historically, the regulated sector has been limited to the banking community; it has been widely acknowledged for some time that banks are on the front line in the fight against money laundering. However, over time and in many jurisdictions, the regulated sector has expanded to include nonbanking financial institutions—such as insurance companies, investment managers, and other participants in the financial sector—stemming in large part from the conventional wisdom that money launderers tend to move their operations into channels where they believe their illicit activities are likely to go undetected.

Allied with the conviction that the AML environment needed change was the perception that previous efforts had been impeded by inadequate legislation and enforcement powers, particularly in cases involving foreign persons, foreign banks, and foreign countries. To this end, the act widened the AML regime to incorporate the nonbanking financial sector, including investment managers and broker/dealers.

If a company is regulated for AML purposes, it is likely that, at a minimum, the company needs to introduce systems and controls designed to minimize and frustrate money laundering. Although the particular requirements vary by jurisdiction, there are five main areas that regulated institutions need to address to varying degrees. The purpose of underlying programs that incorporate these five concerns is to know your customer (KYC) and to monitor transactions in such a way that for more detailed inquiry, apparently unusual transactions can be pulled out of the normal processing flow either before or after they are executed.

Reflection Menu

1. In money laundering, a front doing legitimate business provides cover for delivery and transportation related to illegal activity. TRUE [ ] FALSE [ ]

2. A front business can be a very ineffective way to launder money because it provides a safe place for organising and managing criminal activity. TRUE [ ] FALSE [ ]

3. The money-laundering triad include the following EXCEPT:
    a. placement, layering, and integration
    b. placement, layering, justification, and investment.
    c. placement, layering, integration, and investment.

4. Which of the following is not among the three methods most commonly used to hide assets or launder money through a front business?

    a. Overstatement of reported revenues
    b. Overstatement of reported expenses
    c. Balance sheet laundering
    d. Post balance sheet laundering

(For the answers, please turn to Appendix A)

6 Organized Financial Crimes

Introduction

Most criminologists have adopted the distinction first made by Marshall B. Clinard and Richard Quinney between *occupational crime* and *organizational crime*. Organizational crime is that committed by businesses, particularly corporations, and government. Occupational crime involves offences against the law by individuals in the course of their occupation. An antitrust offence would be an organizational crime, accepting or offering bribes an occupational offence.

Organizational crime occurs in the context of complex relationships and expectations among boards of directors, executives, and managers on the one hand and among parent corporations, corporate divisions, and subsidiaries on the other. White-collar crime is distinguished from lower socio-economic crimes in terms of the structure of the violation and the fact that administrative and civil penalties are more likely to be used as punishment than are criminal penalties.

While corporations cannot be jailed, they may be confined. Most corporate lawbreakers are handled by government regulatory agencies. Enforcement measures might include warning letters, consent agreements or decrees not to repeat the violation; orders of regulatory agencies to compel compliance, seizure, or recall of goods; administrative or civil monetary penalties; and court injunctions to refrain from further violations.

The Swiss banking system has often been accused of offering a hiding place for stolen or looted money, providing a screen for stock manipulations and shady promoters and helping tax evaders conceal both income and assets. Deposits in Swiss banks are often laundered to obscure their illegal origins, and then through new commercial transactions the money is made legal and therefore concealed from tax authorities.

Corporate Organization and Crimes

Corporate Organization and Criminal Behaviour

Corporate offences take place in a context of complex relationships and expectations in an organizational setting. It is often difficult to distinguish which corporate participants ought to be held personally responsible for the wrongdoing. Many offences are the result of myriad decisions made by different persons and passing through a chain of command. Not uncommonly, when corporate acts are contrary to the law, upper-level executives take pains to avoid learning what is going on so as to avoid responsibility if a scheme is uncovered. In some corporations, there is one executive, well-paid, who is only half in jest referred to as the "vice president in charge of going to jail."

The law largely treats corporations as persons. They make more inviting prosecutor targets than individuals, most notably because they have deeper pockets and can be heavily fined to repay losses that have been inflicted on persons or on the society in general.

Government regulatory agencies oversee corporate performance in areas assigned to them by Parliament. Typically, the lawmakers enact a statute that is deliberately vague, allowing the enforcement agency to develop its own enforcement guidelines within the boundaries of the parliamentary authorisation. The agencies will sometimes seek to expand the reach of the law by selecting notably egregious cases for litigation and appeal, thereby anticipating a favourable ruling on what is fundamentally a somewhat novel interpretation of their mandate.

The Image of the Corporation

Large corporations have contributed significantly to industrial and commercial development throughout the world. Their size and resources enable them to organise and coordinate production and distribution. The capital resources of a large corporation provide it with the ability to develop, adopt, and alter technology on a mammoth scale. A considerable portion of the population has been accorded a high standard of living because of corporate activity.

At the same time, large corporations have the power to influence the manner in which laws are written and to commit acts that can inflict serious harm upon the population. They can hire lobbyists and lawyers who manipulate definitions of wrongdoing in the corporations' interests.

The very largeness and remoteness of the corporation from most of us is part of the reason that many of us traditionally have a love-hate attitude toward such organizations. We admire and desire their products, but we are uneasy about their power, a power that tends to be used single-mindedly in the pursuit of profits. Thomas Hobbes, a seventeenth-century English political philosopher, stands out in the crowd that has been scornful of corporations.

Clinard and Yeager

In a comprehensive study of corporate law-breaking, Marshall Clinard and Peter Yeager found that 1,553 white-collar crime cases had been filed against the 562 Fortune 500 US businesses whose records they scrutinised for a two-year period. Some 60 percent of the firms had at least one case against them; for those companies, the average number of violations was 4.4. The oil, pharmaceutical, and motor vehicle industries were the most likely to be charged for wrongdoing, a matter that may be a function of enforcement priorities or a true reflection of their activities. The costs of corporate crimes not only include financial losses, but also injuries, deaths, and health hazards. Such crimes destroy public confidence in businesses and hurt the image of corporations. Clinard and Yeager say price-fixing offences victimise the consumer and federal, provincial, state, and municipal governments while income tax crimes deprive the government and those dependent on it of needed revenue.

Clinard and Yeager believe that corporate violations are increasingly difficult to discover, investigate, or prosecute successfully because of their growing complexity and intricacy. This is particularly true, they believe, of anti-trust cases, foreign payoffs, computer fraud, and illegal political contributions. In the last category, some corporations pay bonuses to their executives, with the understanding that part of that reward will be turned over to the coffers of a candidate that the corporation favours.

Criminal activities involving corporations are often rooted in organizational subcultures and values developed over time. A particularly comprehensive examination of how matters of life and death become embedded in routine decision-making and ultimately can lead to tragedy is provided in a book titled *The Challenger Space Shuttle Disaster* by Diane Vaughan.

Legal responses have been slow and ineffectual when dealing with economic organizational change. The law has emphasised the role of the individual actor in criminality but has not examined the role of the organization in crime. Criminal activities are often rooted in organizational subculture and attitudes developed over time and cannot be traced to individuals or groups within the organization. While individuals still carry out the criminal enterprise, their attitudes and characteristics are of little importance, as an organization will replace those employees unwilling to participate in a criminal activity.

Opportunities for Unlawful Organizational Behaviour

Organizational Structure

Complex companies provide a structure that can foster misbehavior. They provide many settings where misconduct is possible. They isolate those settings in departments and in locations around a city, the country, or the world. The isolation, in turn, means that information about what one part of a company is doing may be unknown in another part. All this reduces the risk that misbehavior will be detected and punished. The larger a company grows, the more specialized its subunits tend to become. An internally diversified company may have few employees who fully understand the detailed workings.

Specialized departments in a large firm compete for resources not only with other firms but with departments in their own firm. The need to outperform not only other businesses but other units within their own business can generate sufficient pressure to lead to misconduct. Vaughan notes that departments often have survival concerns that conflict with the larger interests of an organization. When given a chance to make decisions, she writes, lower-level managers will tend to act not in the interest of the firm but in the interests of their departments.

Specialization also hides illegal activities, especially where a firm's tasks are kept separate and unrelated. Employees cannot garner knowledge about all the particulars of how a firm works. This protects a company from the effects of personnel turnover and leaks of information because no one can offer much more than a piece of the jigsaw puzzle that makes up the company picture. The same secrecy, however, raises the chances for misconduct.

Companies spell out rules in a common language to decide how tasks will be performed and to create common bonds that will facilitate decision-making. But a company's ability to coordinate all its activities varies considerably. Vaughan writes that organizational growth naturally leads to a progressive loss of control over departments. Executives cannot hope to keep track of all the units in a huge company and must rely on subordinates to carry out policy. Vaughan states that when the distance between top executives and subordinate units grows to a sufficient level "authority leakage" results. Such leakage means the company has become too unwieldy for an executive to enforce rules at all levels. "The organization, in short," Vaughan writes, "can diversify beyond the capability of those at the top to master it."

Such leakage allows subsidiaries, company researchers, accountants, or other departments to engage in misconduct without any assurance that internal controls will check the behavior. In some cases, as with computer crime, detecting misconduct might be beyond the ability of most employees. Conversely, authority leakage and specialization can also lead an organization to comply with societal rules even when the organizational pressures lean toward misconduct.

Does the existence of authority imply a loss of company control? While a company that cannot steer its employees' behavior might be viewed as irrational or incompetent, the ability to control information flow from top to bottom may not be possible. Research and theory suggest, to the contrary, that information is processed selectively through a company in ways that tend to protect the interests of departments and to promote efficiency.

Sometimes censorship of information promotes a company's interests. In other cases, "need to know" policies or ignorance of rules that are irrelevant to a department leads to inefficiencies. All these tendencies restrict information flow and create opportunities for one unit in a company to act outside the knowledge of other units. Censorship policies may originate in any part of a company and hide matters throughout the organization.

The tiered structure of most organizations obscures personal responsibility and tends to spread it throughout the company. Thus, determining where a decision to engage in misconduct originated can be difficult. Author John E. Conklin put it this way: "The delegation of responsibility and unwritten orders keep those at the top of the corporate structure remote from the consequences of their decisions and orders, much as the heads of organised crime families remain 'untouchable' by law."

Criminogenic Organizational Structures

Sociologist Edward Gross has asserted that all organizations are inherently criminogenic (that is, prone to committing crime), though not necessarily criminal. Gross makes this assertion because of the reliance on "the bottom line." Without necessarily meaning to, organizations can invite fraud as a means of obtaining goals. Criminologist Oliver Williamson noted that because of a department's concern with reaching its goals, managers might well tend to maximise their department's own interests to the detriment of the organization.

Organizations can also be criminogenic because they encourage loyalty.

According to Diane Vaughan, the reasons are that

- The organization tends to recruit and attract similar individuals.
- Rewards are given out to those who display characteristics of the "company man." Long-term loyalty is encouraged through company retirement and benefits.
- Loyalty is encouraged through social interaction, such as company parties and social functions.
- Frequent transfers and long working hours encourage isolation from other groups.
- Specialized job skills can discourage personnel from seeking employment elsewhere.

This in turn causes company personnel to sometimes perceive that the organization might be worth committing crime to maintain and further its goals. The use of formal and informal rewards and punishments, plus social activities and pressures to participate, link an employee's needs and goals to the success of the company. Society places value on the reputation of the company for which one works, reinforcing the link between an individual and corporate goals. When a company achieves its goals, its employees prosper. In short, the interests of an organization and its employees coincide, and that situation may set the stage for unlawful conduct by individuals on the organization's behalf.

Vaughan writes that organizational processes create "an internal moral and intellectual world" that causes individuals to identify with organizational goals. Company survival comes to mean individual survival, and when resources become scarce, the incentive to misbehave increases. Of course, not all agents will act unlawfully on a company's behalf, and how any employee behaves will be linked to factors that might not be related to the world of the organization.

When the structural pressure to commit fraud exists, a firm often cannot unite its agents in such activities. At least three factors prevent such unity. First, the pressure to commit fraud might not affect departments in a company equally. A sales department that must meet certain goals to generate profits will feel different competitive pressure than a product development department in the same company that is running smoothly. Some parts of companies might never experience pressure to cheat, and members of those departments will have no motivation to engage in misconduct on a firm's behalf.

Second, even in high-pressure departments, some employees will not have knowledge of the difficulty of obtaining needed resources. An employee will have no motivation to commit fraud unless he has full information about an organization's goals and how the department can achieve them. In other words, an employee usually needs a high degree of responsibility for a company's success, as well as the ability to bring about those goals, before a chance to engage in misbehavior can occur.

Third, outside societal behaviour can produce values that conflict with those learned in an organizational environment. For example, fraternal or professional associations impart their own values to employees that may not coincide with a specific corporate code of honor. When faced with conflicting norms, Vaughan writes, employees will make their choices based on the rewards and punishments they perceive to accompany the alternatives. Where misbehavior is seen as too costly, it will not occur. Where an organization provides sufficient rewards to overcome the fear of punishment, misbehaviour may occur despite competing norms. The amount of information an employee has will affect the decision on which way to go, as will an individual's financial and social dependence on the firm.

The mere fact that corporate and individual goals are often joined in organizations does not necessarily create a climate for illegal actions. As with any major decision, complexities often enter the picture. Temptations vary not only among departments but within them. The availability of information and individual risk-reward assessments may generate lawful behaviour that resists organizational pressures to violate the law, as well as unlawful behaviour in the face of organizational pressures to comply. Put plainly, the likelihood that organizational processes will generate misbehavior is highly variable and cannot currently be measured with any degree of precision.

In explaining how employees are taught to make decisions that are correct from a corporation's standpoint, Drucker said a natural tendency exists in every large-scale organization to discourage initiative and encourage conformity. Madden and Margolis say corporations lead new managers through an initiation period designed to weaken their ties with external groups, including their own families, and encourage a feeling of dependence on and attachment to the corporation.

Geis found that quite often, individuals are trained in illegal behaviour as part of the occupational role. Schrager and Short say criminal behavior stems more from the roles an employee is expected to fulfil than from individual pathology. Many executives know their behavior is illegal but tend to justify their behavior as simply common practice in the business world. Clinard and Yeager believed that in rationalizing their behaviour, corporations follow a general tendency to obey laws selectively, i.e., obeying according to situational needs and determined by factors like social class and occupation.

Sutherland demonstrated that corporate executives are insulated from those who might disagree with their beliefs because they associate almost exclusively with people who are pro-business, politically conservative, and generally opposed to government regulation. Silk and Vogel found that certain beliefs exist in the business world about government intervention in business and defend the corporation's acts to violate, such as "all legal measures proposed constitute government interference with the free enterprise system."

A problem common to many large corporations with intricate hierarchical structures tends to be a split between what the upper levels believe is going on below and the actual procedures being carried out. Clinard and Yeager say that the chief executive officer of a corporation is often isolated, and messages transmitted down the line tend to become distorted. Clinard and Yeager found that all levels of the corporation might often agree to perpetuate the lack of full information, for the key to any successful conspiracy to violate the law probably lies in the fact that the higher-ups do not inquire about what is going on and the lower levels do not tell them.

Often in corporations, no single individual at the highest levels may make a decision alone to market a faulty product or take short-cuts on product testing, Clinard and Yeager say. Instead, decisions are made in small steps at each level possibly without any awareness of the illegal and potentially dangerous result. McCaghy says profit pressure is "the single most compelling factor behind deviance by industry, whether it be price fixing, the destruction of competition or the misrepresentation of a product," such as making a shoddy product that will wear out and need to be replaced. Clinard and Yeager say certain industries, such as the drug and chemical businesses, have such severe competition and strong profit drives due to demands for continual development of new products that they may feel pressured to falsify test data, market new products before their full effects are known, or engage in unethical sales techniques that can have disastrous effects on human beings and the environment.

Corporate Executives and Criminal Liability

Many of the ethical and legal problems of a corporation result from the corporate structure that separates ownership from management. Typical large corporations are administered by a group of salaried managers, where the board of directors exercises little direct power other than hiring or firing the managers, and so corporate managers have great autonomy over decisions regarding production, investment, pricing, and marketing.

Executives tend to believe that their jobs are at risk if they cannot show a profit to higher management or the board of directors, and often, they are. Clinard and Yeager hold that if goals for managers are set too high, the employee then confronts a hard choice of risking being thought incompetent or taking unethical or even illegal shortcuts.

According to Clinard and Yeager, corporations often try to protect their executives from liability by agreeing to pay fines, court costs, and attorney's fees with corporate funds; bonuses or raises or liability insurance might offer protection to officers or directors. Generally, executive compensation and tenure remain untouched. There is much difficulty in criminal prosecution of executives because corporate violations are usually far more complex than conventional crimes. Also, the complexity of the legal proof required allows businessmen to test the limits of the law.

Businessmen might have sought legal advice on loopholes in the law before committing the offence, Clinard and Yeager say, which may be cited as evidence that the executives thought they were in legal compliance. Businessmen can hire highly skilled lawyers who present arguments as to the client's lack of previous convictions or unlikelihood of becoming a repeat offender as well as being able to cite numerous precedents where businessmen were charged but not imprisoned for similar violations.

Corporate offenders are usually not imprisoned with ordinary criminals but are usually incarcerated in institutions designed for low-risk inmates with short sentences, presumably for the corporate offender's own physical safety. Justifications used in arguing against a prison sentence for corporate offenders include

1. age and poor health;
2. personal and family reasons;
3. extent of punishment already suffered by virtue of being indicted;
4. offence was not immoral;
5. defendant has no prior record, is not a threat to society, and has been a prominent citizen active in community affairs;

6. incarceration would accomplish nothing (no benefit to society);
7. defendant is repentant; and
8. victimization of corporate executives solely because of their position.

Some corporate offenders are given community service as punishment, such as giving speeches about their offences to businesses and civic groups, working in programs designed to aid the poor, or helping former ordinary criminal offenders secure job pledges from businesses.

Management Behaviour

Brenner and Molander found that superiors are the primary influence in unethical decision making. Therefore, the use of sanctions to accomplish compliance with the law is but one of the various forces operating within a corporation encouraging or opposing violations of law. Stone found that the success of law enforcement "ultimately depends upon its consistency with and reinforcement of the organization's rules for advancement and reward, its customs, conventions, and morals." He maintains that if the law is too much at odds with the corporation's "culture," employees will tend to cover up their tracks rather than change their behaviour.

Corporations also argue "regulation is faulty because most government regulations are incomprehensible and too complex." Conklin found that anti-trust laws are seen as inconsistent, hypocritical, poorly defined, and rarely enforced. Therefore, most regulations must be written in detail to cover as many contingencies as possible. Silk and Vogel found several other actions used by business to rationalise conduct:

• Government regulations are unjustified because the additional costs of regulations and bureaucratic procedures cut heavily into profits.

- Regulation is unnecessary because the matters being regulated are unimportant.
- Although some corporate violations involve millions of dollars, the damage is so diffused among a large number of consumers that individually there is little loss.
- Violations are caused by economic necessity; they aim to protect the value of stock to ensure an adequate return for stockholders and to protect the job security of employees by ensuring the financial stability of the corporation.

John Braithwaite is a researcher in white-collar crime at Australian National University in Canberra. Braithwaite views white-collar crime as a product of the corporate subculture. In Braithwaite's view, corporations will turn to crime as a result of "blocked opportunities." Because white-collar crime can exist only in secrecy, deviant subcultures develop (conspiracy among executives, for example), lines of communication are not allowed to develop, and people operate within spheres of responsibility.

Controlling Organizational Crime

Clinard and Yeager believe corporations that do violate and those that do not are distinguished by "corporate cultures" or ethical climates, which is the degree to which a corporation has made the choice to be unethical or not, to disregard the interests of the consumer and the public, and to disobey the laws that regulate its specific industry.

Efforts to control corporate crime follow three approaches: voluntary change in corporate attitudes and structure; strong intervention of the political state to force changes in corporate structure, accompanied by legal measures to deter or punish; or consumer action. Voluntary changes would involve the development of stronger business ethics and certain corporate organizational reforms; government controls might involve federal corporate chartering, deconcentration, and divestiture, larger and more effective enforcement staffs, stiffer penalties, wider use of publicity as a sanction, and possibly the nationalisation of corporations; and consumer group pressures may be exerted through lobbying, selective buying, boycotts, and the establishment of large consumer cooperatives.

Clinard and Yeager suggest that a wide, comprehensive industrial code of ethics, which many businessmen favor, would be of great help when a businessman wished to refuse an unethical request, would help define more clearly the limits of acceptable or ethical conduct, would improve the ethical climate of the industry, and would serve to reduce cutthroat practices where competition is intense. Greater stockholder involvement might enable greater corporate compliance with the law, but in actuality, it is the management staff who runs the company and makes the decisions and the stockholders are primarily concerned with stock growth and dividends.

In some cases, critical information dealing with possible law violations simply fails to reach the board of directors. New board members are usually nominated by the board and routinely approved by stockholders, making boards self-perpetuating. Board members are often drawn from management. Many corporations now employ outside directors and/or representatives of the public interest, much like the practice abroad of naming union representatives to boards. These public members represent the public and consumer concerns, ascertain whether the corporation is complying with the law, assist and maintain corporate public responsibility, help monitor the internal management system to discover faulty workmanship and report it to the board, serve as liaisons with government agencies with respect to legislation or standards, and serve as a hotline to receive information about deviance.

Clinard and Yeager found that mass media publicity about law violations probably represents the most feared consequence of sanctions imposed on a corporation. Publicity can also inform the public about the operation of regulatory controls and enable people to understand the purposes of the controls. Informal publicity is ordinarily carried as news items from the media while formal publicity is a requirement that a corporation must, as part of an enforcement action, publish an advertisement or some other statement acknowledging a violation and that corrective measures are being taken.

If illegal behavior consistently resulted in decreased patronage or even consumer boycotts, consumer pressure would be an effective tool in the control of illegal corporate behavior. However, say Clinard and Yeager, it appears to not be very effective. Consumers are often unaware when a corporation's products are unsafe or when it has been violating anti-trust laws or polluting the environment. Without organised behavior, a consumer's withdrawal of individual patronage is generally ineffective.

Many corporations settle charges without admitting or denying guilt by consenting to either an administrative or a court-ordered decree banning future violations. In a consent agreement, the corporation reaches an understanding with the government agency not to violate the regulation again. In a decree, the agreement is ratified by the court.

Sporkin says consent decrees have enabled the appointment of special officers to investigate and pursue claims against erring management and others on behalf of the corporation and its shareholders, the placement of people independent of management and not previously associated with the company on the board of directors, and the appointment of special review or audit committees. A problem with consent orders, however, is that frequently, they are not followed up to find out whether the terms imposed are being met.

Criminal fines and civil and administrative penalties against corporations are forms of monetary penalties. For completion, criminal cases average about one year from indictment to conviction, civil actions about two years, and administrative cases about four months.

Criminal action against corporations is difficult to initiate because generally, government agencies are dependent upon the records of the corporation and its ability or willingness to furnish needed information. Not all experts agree that monetary penalties are appropriate. For example, a $25 million fine to a pauper would have no effect. One novel approach to punishing corporations was proposed by Coffee (1978). He advocates stock dilution or "equity fining." Under this approach, the convicted corporation would issue additional shares of stock to the state equal to the cash value of a fine. The state could collect the equity shares and well them, trade them, or keep them for their earnings power. With respect to monetary penalties, some argue that these sanctions are limited to a person's own worth and therefore have limited utility. In 1992, the US Congress implemented the corporate sentencing guidelines, providing up to $290 million in fines for illegal corporate behavior.

Some of the criteria considered when deciding to bring criminal action against a corporation are the degree of loss to the public, the duration of the violation, the level of complicity by high corporate managers, the frequency of the violation, evidence of intent to violate, evidence of extortion, the degree of notoriety endangered by the media, precedent in law, a history of serious violations by the corporation, deterrence potential, and the degree of cooperation demonstrated by the corporation.

The Enforcement Effort: Preventing and Reducing Fraud

While the issues involved in the enforcement effort provide a context in which to assess the efforts to control white-collar crime, actual techniques of prevention need to be discussed. There are many theories about enforcement, sanctions, and punishments that are a part of controlling white-collar crime. Enforcement strategies include two main theories: compliance and deterrence.

Compliance

Compliance hopes to achieve conformity to the law without having to detect, process, or penalise violators. Compliance systems provide economic incentives for voluntary compliance to the laws and use administrative efforts to control violations before they occur.

Compliance strategies have been criticised by some criminologists. These experts believe that compliance has little effect, as sanctions are imposed after the infraction occurs. Since economic penalties are common punishments for violators, these penalties amount to little more than the proverbial "slap on the wrist" in the case of large, wealthy corporations.

Deterrence

As a strategy to control crime, *deterrence* is designed to detect law violations, determine who is responsible, and penalise offenders in order to deter future violations. Deterrence systems try to control the immediate behavior of individuals, not the long-term behaviors targeted by compliance systems.

Deterrence theory assumes that humans are rational in their behavior patterns. Humans seek profit and pleasure while they try to avoid pain. Deterrence assumes that an individual's propensity toward lawbreaking is in inverse proportion to the perceived probability of negative consequences.

Increased Enforcement

Formal levels of current enforcement in white-collar crime are, by all measures, extremely low. One view holds that increased enforcement can only come with a complete and total revision of the criminal justice system. Currently, people have little fear of detection because they know that the police and courts cannot keep up with the pace of criminal offences. It is not necessary or even desirable to advocate longer prison sentences for offenders because we do not have the courts and jails to accommodate them. Perhaps a better plan would be to sacrifice the severity of punishment for certainty. Until potential offenders have the perception that they will be caught and punished, we cannot expect a reversal of the crime trend.

Fraud Prevention Programs

Although the government can provide incentives for organizations to prevent fraud, ultimately, it is up to management to institute prevention programs. The Fraud Prevention Programs chapter describes methods whereby management can institute policies and procedures to help detect and prevent fraud.

Examples of Organized Financial Crime

Advance Fee and Internet Fraud

Once again, criminals based in Nigeria appear to be the pioneers and remain very prominent in this area. These criminals are noted for the most notorious type of advanced fraud the 419 named after the section in the Nigerian Criminal Penal code. The 419's are by definition attempts to obtain pre-payments for goods and services that do not actually exist or which the fraudsters does not actually deliver. One of the key features of the 419 fraud is that the fraudsters propose a service that is clearly illegal such as laundering illicit funds via the victim's bank account.

Loan Sharking

Loan-sharking is the lending of money at higher rates than the law allows. Many people get involved with loan sharks. Gamblers borrow in order to pay gambling losses; narcotics users borrow to purchase drugs; and businessmen borrow when legitimate credit channels are closed. Loan sharks menace both white- and blue-collar workers as well as small and large corporations. Employees have agreed to disclose corporate secrets; leave warehouses unlocked, steal securities, ship stolen goods, and pass along information about customers, which sets the business up for burglaries. Officers of both small and large corporations are forced to turn over control of their companies to organized crime. Loan-sharking is identified as extortionate credit transactions. The elements of extortionate credit transactions are:

- The extension of credit would be unenforceable through civil judicial processes against the debtor.
- The extension of credit was made at a rate of interest in excess of 45 percent per annum.
- The extension of credit was collected or attempted to be collected by extortionate means.
- The interest or similar charges exceeded $100.

Labour Racketeering

Labor unions provide many methods for illicit gains:

- Kickbacks from employers for favorable contracts and labor peace are common, as is extortion.
- The unions can provide a vehicle for embezzlement. Organized crime syndicates use excessive or fictitious salaries or expenses, nonworking associates, or personal work done by union officers or employees. Professional or legal services are used to benefit union officials or employees. Sometimes they make donations to organizations for the benefit of a union official or employee.
- Welfare and pension funds provide vehicles for kickbacks from insurance agents and organized crime investments and loans.

The audit program and techniques are many and varied when dealing with union racketeering.

Stock Fraud and Manipulation

Some criminals use stock and bond fraud schemes to make illicit gains. They use counterfeit stock certificates as collateral on loans. They set up dummy corporations to sell worthless stock in boiler room operations. A legitimate corporation can be taken over and sold back and forth between insiders so as to highly inflate the market price of the stock. After the stock is sold at highly inflated prices, the company would be abandoned, and the stock allowed drop to the correct market value. Stock and bond fraud is a complex and sophisticated area. Extremely detailed investigation and analysis are required. The investigation requires analysis of transactions before, during, and after the scheme to determine the trends.

Nonprofit Organization Fraud

This type of fraud is primarily a tax fraud even though other types of fraud are also committed. In some cases, the victims do not know that they have been defrauded, while in other cases, the victims suffer both great financial and emotional losses. The Internal Revenue Service, as well as many state laws, allow various types of organizations to operate without paying taxes, obtaining permits and licenses, and exempt them from various laws and regulations.

Religious institutions, social clubs, paternal organizations, and various charities operate to help or benefit their members or the community in which they operate.

These nonprofit organizations are very beneficial to members and the community; however, there are individuals who operate or control these organizations for their own benefit, and this is illegal.

Tax Evasion

The federal and state governments in many countries have laws that make it a felony for those who willfully attempt to evade or defeat any tax. The crime of willful tax evasion is completed when the false or fraudulent return is willfully and knowingly filed. Tax evasion must be proved by an affirmative act. The willful failure to collect or pay tax is a felony. Likewise, it must be proved by an affirmative act. The net worth, nondeductible expenditure method is the one most used by the Internal Revenue Service and states with individual income tax laws. Voluntary disclosures by taxpayers of intentional violation of tax laws prior to the initiation of an investigation do not ensure that the government will not recommend criminal prosecution. There is no requirement that returns be made under oath. The law merely requires that returns contain a declaration that they are made under the penalties of perjury. Perjury is considered a felony. Any person who willfully delivers or discloses any list, return, account, statement, or other document that is known to be fraudulent or false is committing a crime. The federal government classifies this as a misdemeanor; however, many states classify this as a felony.

The taxpayer is responsible for the correctness of any return filed, even if he pays a preparer. If the preparer has willfully prepared a false return, then he or she can be criminally prosecuted.

Corporate Raiding

Corporate raiding involves individuals or organizations that take over business entities for the purpose of exploiting the business assets for gain. These corporate raids may be for the control of the industry or for personal gain. Generally, corporate raiding involves either violations of the Antitrust Act or a combination of other offenses, e.g., embezzlement, pension fraud, bankruptcy fraud, or stock fraud or manipulation.

Restraint of Trade

Restraint of trade is a violation by corporate decision makers on behalf of their organizations. In USA, the major federal statute involved is the Sherman Antitrust Act of 1890. It was designed to curb the threat to a competitive, free-enterprise economy posed by the spread of trusts and monopolies to combine or form monopolies. There are three principal methods of restraint of trade:

- Consolidation, so as to obtain a monopoly position
- Price fixing to achieve price uniformity
- Price discrimination, in which higher prices are charged to some customers and lower ones to others

For those corporate decision makers, restraint of trade makes sense in that the less competition a corporation has and the greater control over prices, the larger the profits. However, small and independent businesses will lose business, and the public at large will face higher prices and loss of discretionary buying power. The most common violations are price fixing and price discrimination.

Money laundering

Money laundering is the illegal handling of the proceeds of one or more criminal offence, with the objective of obscuring its origins so that it can be enjoyed by the offenders or used to further more crime. It is a crime that requires other crimes to have been committed described as "predicate offences." It represents a vital support function to most organised crime and terrorism and is, therefore, among the most important of the crimes addressed in this report.

Money laundering may be committed by commercial concerns, mostly at the smaller end of the scale, as a side business to their legitimate activities. For example, cash businesses, such as retail shops or clubs and restaurants, can add illegal funds to their normal takings for banking purposes and refund them in more apparently legitimate form to the original criminal, after taking a profit margin. Larger entities, such as financial institutions, can turn a blind eye to suspect funds, in order to maximise their business.

Agencies Involved in the Fighting Tax and Other Financial Crimes

Financial crime covers a broad range of offences, including tax evasion and tax fraud, money laundering, corruption, insider trading, bankruptcy fraud, and terrorist financing. Several different government agencies may be involved in the different stages of tackling financial crimes. These stages include the prevention, detection, investigation, and prosecution of these crimes, as well as the recovery of the proceeds of crime. Several agencies, which may be involved at these different stages, include police forces and prosecution authorities, which have a visible role in law enforcement. They also include agencies such as tax administrations and financial supervisory bodies, which have access to significant information about individuals, corporations, and financial transactions.

There is no single approach to how countries structure these agencies and allocate competences among them. Activities that are the responsibility of a particular agency in one country may be the responsibility of a different agency in a second country. Similarly, some countries may establish independent agencies to carry out activities that in other countries are the responsibility of a larger body.

Understanding these differences is important in appreciating the implications of similarities and differences between different countries' arrangements for inter-agency cooperation. Which agency has responsibility for a particular activity will directly impact on the availability of instruments for international cooperation. For example, whether responsibility for investigating tax fraud lies with the tax administration or rather with the police will directly influence the cooperative arrangements required to facilitate these investigations. In general terms, there are a number of key agencies in the fight against tax crimes and other financial crimes and their roles are briefly described below.

A. Tax Administration

A country's tax administration is generally responsible for the assessment and collection of taxes on behalf of the government. This involves gathering and processing information on individuals and corporations subject to tax, including personal details, property, investments, financial transactions, and business operations. A tax administration often employs large numbers of trained specialists and investigators with experience in auditing and analysing financial data and investigating suspicious or anomalous transactions. Tax administrations may have extensive powers to access information. In most countries, the tax administration plays a central role in deterring and detecting tax crime. Once a suspected tax crime has been identified, the extent to which the tax administration is involved in the investigation and prosecution varies.

B. Customs Administration

Customs administrations are responsible for the assessment and collection of customs duties. In many countries, they also have responsibility for other taxes and duties, including excise duties and indirect taxes, such as sales taxes and VAT. Customs administrations hold information about cross-border flows of money and goods, as well as details of individual businesses. Customs administrations may be established as separate agencies or as part of a joint tax and customs administration.

C. Financial Intelligence Unit

Since the early 1990s, Financial Intelligence Units (FIUs) have been central to national strategies to combat money laundering and terrorist financing. FIUs are typically the central agencies responsible for receiving (and as permitted requesting), analysing and disseminating (*core functions* of a FIU) to the competent authorities, disclosures of financial information (i) concerning suspected proceeds of crime and potential financing of terrorism or (ii) required by national legislation or regulation, in order to combat money laundering and terrorism financing. FIUs may have further responsibilities regarding the gathering and analysis of information on movements of funds and other suspicious activities (*e.g.,* cash transaction reports, wire transfer reports, and other threshold based declarations/disclosures). Beyond its core functions and based on national legislation, the FIU may also be responsible for regulating and/or supervising certain financial institutions and Designated Non-Financial Businesses and Professions (DNFBPs) to ensure compliance with anti–money laundering/combating the financing of terrorism (AML/CFT) legislation.

D. Police

The police force is typically the primary agency in a country with responsibility to enforce criminal law, protect property, and prevent civil unrest in civilian matters. Due to the specialist nature of the different categories of financial crime, some police forces have set up specific teams to deal with this type of offence. Other countries may have several distinct police forces with responsibility for different types of criminal activity.

E. Prosecution authorities

In the majority of countries, there is a single national prosecution authority responsible for prosecuting most criminal offences, including tax crimes and other financial crimes. Within the national prosecution authority, in some instances, there are specialist divisions or prosecutors dealing with tax crimes, money laundering, and other financial offences. In a small number of countries, offences may be prosecuted directly by investigative agencies.

F.   Financial supervisors

Financial supervisors, including central banks, are typically responsible for the proper and effective regulation and supervision of specified categories of financial institutions. This promotes monetary and financial stability and is aimed to ensure efficient functioning in the financial sector. Financial supervisors may achieve these goals through regulation, supervision, and enforcement, including the investigation of potential legislative or regulatory breaches.

G.   Specialist law enforcement agencies

Many countries have specialist law enforcement agencies with responsibility for investigating and, in some cases, prosecuting specific types of criminal offence.

7 Tracing Illicit Transactions

Introduction

Interviewing in order to obtain financial data involves the systematic questioning of people who have knowledge of the events, the people involved, and the physical evidence surrounding the case. Financial interviewing is not unlike other kinds of interviewing. However, evidence often develops in bits and pieces that, when viewed separately, might appear to lead nowhere. Frustration is common, and tactics and techniques might have to be modified. Diligence, patience, and persistence are essential for successful results. The following is a checklist of general information that can be covered in the financial interview.

Comprehensive Guidelines for Information to Be Collected in Financial Interviews

Identification
- Full name
- Alias
- Reason for alias

Birth
- Date and place of birth
- Citizenship
- Father's name; living? (If deceased, when?)
- Mother's name; living? (If deceased, when?)

Address during pertinent years
- Resident address; phone number
- Business address; phone number
- Other present or prior address(es)
- Marital status; if married, date and place of marriage
- If divorced, when and where
- Spouse's maiden name
- Spouse's parents; living? (If deceased, when?)
- Children's names and ages; other dependents

Occupation
- Present occupation
- Company name and address
- Present salary
- Length of time employed
- Additional employment
- Prior occupations
- Spouse's occupation

General background
- Physical health
- Mental health
- Education
- Professional qualifications
- Military service
- Passport, Social Security, and/or social insurance numbers (for identification purposes)
- Ever been investigated for financial crimes?
- Ever been arrested?
- Ever filed bankruptcy? If so, who acted as receiver/trustee?
- Hobbies and interests

Financial institutions (business and personal)
- Financial institution accounts
- Safe deposit boxes (request inventory)—in whose name; contents; does anyone else have access?

- Credit cards
- Trusts—beneficiary, donor, or trustee
- Mutual funds or other securities owned
- Brokers—currency exchanges used
- Life insurance
- Indirect dealings (e.g., through lawyers or accountants)
- Cashier's cheques
- Money orders, bank drafts, traveller's cheques

Source of income
- Salaries, wages, business receipts
- Interest and dividends
- Sale of securities
- Rents and royalties
- Pensions, trusts, annuities, etc.
- Gifts (money, property, etc.)
- Inheritances
- Loans
- Mortgages
- Sales of assets
- Municipal bond interest
- Insurance settlements
- Damages from legal actions
- Any other source of funds, ever

Net income and expenditures
- Current cash on hand, including cash in safe deposit boxes, but not cash in bank accounts
- Location of current cash
- Largest amount of cash ever on hand; location
- End-of-year cash
- Notes receivable
- Mortgages receivable
- Life insurance policies
- Automobiles
- Real estate

- Stocks, bonds, and other securities
- Jewelry, furs
- Airplanes, boats
- Any other assets valued

Liabilities
- Payables
- Loans
- Assets purchased by financing
- Mortgages
- Bonds

Expenditures
- Debt reduction
- Insurance premiums
- Interest expense
- Contributions
- Medical
- Travel
- Real estate and other taxes
- Household wages (e.g., babysitter, housekeeper, gardener)
- Casualty losses

Business operations
- Name and address
- Date organized and nature (corporation, partnership)
- Company or business registration numbers
- Tax identification numbers
- Title and duties
- Reporting arrangements—to and from whom?
- Banking and cash handling arrangements
- Investment—where and when
- Subsidiaries and associates
- Key people

Books and records
- Nature of accounting system (e.g., cash, accrual)
- Period covered
- Location
- Name of person maintaining and controlling
- Types (journal, ledgers, minute books, cancelled cheques, bank statements, invoices, cash)

Business receipts
- Form (electronic, cheque, or cash)
- Are all receipts deposited? Where?
- Are business receipts segregated from personal ones?
- Are expenses ever paid with undeposited receipts?
- Arrangements for foreign currency payments
- Trade finance arrangements, letters of credit, etc.

Direct Methods of Tracing Financial Transactions

Financial Institutions

Forensic investigation professionals should recognize that in most instances, bank records are not readily obtainable. Substantial requirements usually must be met to justify legal process (subpoena, search warrant, and the like), which banks will customarily demand as a condition for disclosure. Preliminary investigation is of the utmost importance to lay the basis for obtaining such records.

The availability of investigative avenues often determines whether a promising fraud examination will grind to a halt or proceed successfully. Legal advice from an attorney should be sought in all such instances. It should also be recognized that bank officials and employees can be questioned by fraud examiners in the same manner as any other potential witnesses and that their responses to proper inquiries might provide important information.

Bank records are perhaps the single most important financial source available to a forensic investigation professional. In addition to their use as evidence for fraud, a bank's records might provide leads on sources of funds, expenditures, and personal affairs. The following information can be of value to fraud examiners seeking information from banks concerning pertinent financial transactions of economic crime perpetrators.

Financial Institution Services

Financial institutions provide a vast array of services including but not limited to:

- Loans and mortgages
- Cheque and savings accounts
- Securities trading
- Mutual fund investments
- Insurance products including life, home, and auto
- Acquisitions and mergers of businesses
- Securitization of lending products
- Merchant Banking joint ventures
- Trust services

Internal Bookkeeping Procedures

The internal record-keeping practices and procedures of banks not only are complex, but also, they constantly are changing because of the growing sophistication of computer technology.

Banks are moving steadily toward an electronic-funds transfer system that could eventually eliminate the use of cheques. Such a system will automatically transfer money from the account of the purchaser to the account of the seller. Paper documents may disappear, but automated audit trails will still exist. Detailed familiarity with the intricacies of internal bank operations is not essential, however, for the fraud examiner to obtain the types of information necessary for investigations. What is essential is the knowledge that records of customers' transactions are maintained and retained.

Types of Bank Records

Bank records identified and discussed below are limited to those of particular interest to Forensic investigation professionals.

Signature Cards

The signature card is the evidence of a contract between the customer and bank. When a depositor opens an account, the bank requires that a signature card be signed. By signing the card, the depositor becomes a party to a contract with the bank under which he accepts all rules and regulations of the bank and authorises the bank to honor his orders for withdrawing funds. For a corporation or a partnership account, the signature card is accompanied by copies of resolutions of the board of directors or partnership agreements naming the person authorised to draw cheques on the accounts.

The signature card is a source of valuable information. Although its form varies, the card usually contains such data as banking connections and the date and amount of the initial deposit. The initial deposit traced through the bank's records may disclose a source of income. The identification of the person who opened the account might be significant, especially if the depositor used an alias.

Many banks investigate the references given by a new customer. They might also make inquiries of various credit reporting agencies. This information is contained in a correspondence file or a credit file that can contain comments of the person who opened the account and might show information given by the depositor when opening the account.

In tracing information about a subject's transactions with the bank, the account number must be used. If it does not appear on the signature card, it can be located in the bank's customer information file. Assigned account numbers are encoded on cheques and deposit slips by means of a system called Magnetic Ink Character Recognition (MICR). When requesting the signature card, the fraud examiner should determine whether the bank maintains any type of central file. Most large banks have a central file that lists all departments with which a customer has had dealings. If the bank has such a file, the examiner does not need to check with each department to obtain information. The subject might at one time have had a bank account that was later closed. Requests for information from a bank about a subject should always include a reference to both active and closed accounts. Records of closed accounts are usually maintained in a separate file.

Negotiated Cheques

Cancelled cheques written by a subject or received from others often provide the fraud examiner/forensic investigation professional with much more than amounts, payees, and endorsees. When looking for assets, a review of the reverse side of negotiated cheques can provide further avenues of investigation and subsequent recovery.

Tracing Cheques

Tracing cheques is facilitated by the use of bank institution numbers. Fraud examiners do not have to understand the internal bookkeeping procedures used by banks. All cheques printed for banking institutions contain a bank institution number. The institution numbers enable a cheque to be routed to the bank of origin. In the process of routing, a trail is left.

Magnetic Ink Character Recognition

Magnetic Ink Character Recognition (MICR) is a machine language and is a cheque design standard to which all banks must conform. Numeric information is printed in magnetic ink on the bottom of bank cheques and other documents. This coding is electronically scanned by computers that convert the magnetic ink notations into electronic impulses readable by a computer. MICR information is printed in groupings called fields. These fields usually the cheque serial number, the branch transit number, the financial institution, and the customer's account number.

The account number field shows the drawer's assigned account number at the bank. When the cheque is processed through the bank, an additional field is added on the right for the amount of the cheque. All cheques, drafts, and similar items that are not encoded with magnetic ink cannot be processed through the clearing system without special handling.

Deposit Slips

The deposit slip is the principal source document for crediting the customer's account. Deposits are first recorded on the deposit slip that usually segregates currency, coins, and cheques. The cheques are listed separately. In some cases, the depositor writes the name of the maker of the cheque on the deposit slip. This might help to identify the source of the cheque. Regardless of the detail contained on a deposit slip, bank record-keeping systems allow deposits to be identified and traced to their sources.

In working with deposit slips, the fraud examiner must remember that sometimes the depositor splits the deposit, meaning only part of the cheque is actually deposited. In these instances, the customer either receives cash or requests that part of the proceeds be applied to a note or interest due to the bank. In some instances, it might be important to determine the total amount of cash and cheques presented for deposit before deductions. When this is the case, the fraud examiner should inquire from the bank how split deposits are handled.

Wire Transfers

Like other transactions, banks keep records of wire transfers. The records will identify who sent the wire, where it was sent, the date, and the amount. If the wire was sent out of the country, tracing the transfer depends on the laws and policies of the country and the receiving institution.

Telegraphic Transfers

On a customer's instructions, funds might be transferred from one bank account to another by wire or telephone. Although the transfer shows as a deposit to the customer's account by means of a credit memo, the detailed records of transfers are usually kept in a special file. If the target has accounts with banks in several cities, the possibility of obtaining funds by wire should be investigated.

Intrabank Transfers

Other departments within a bank can credit the depositor's account for funds collected, such as the proceeds of loans or items held by the bank for collection. Items held by the bank for collection are not always deposited to the customer's account but are sometimes remitted directly to the customer.

Savings Accounts

These are referred to as time deposits because sometimes they are not as readily available to the customer as deposits to a checking account. Funds in a savings account might be subject to a thirty-day notice of withdrawal.

Certificates of Deposit

Certificates of deposit (CDs) are funds left with a bank for a definite period of time, for example, two years, that draw a higher rate of interest than the ordinary savings account.

Bank Ledgers and Bank Statements

Each bank has a bookkeeping department that maintains customer accounts. The bookkeeping department sorts cheques to prepare them for posting; posts cheques to customers' accounts; posts deposits and other credits; takes care of special items, such as "stop payments"; and proves and balances general ledger totals for various types of accounts. How this work is performed depends on whether a manual or a computerized system is used. Different types of records are generated by the two systems. However, a customer's account can be reconstructed under either system. Many banks have centralized process centres that perform this function for several branches.

Bank Statements

In a computerised system, statements are produced periodically (generally monthly) for checking accounts. The bank has digital copies of all statements. It is easier to trace transactions and records with detailed statements showing all transactions. When only summary, or "bobtail," statements are available, all the transactions that make up the statement must be reconstructed.

Savings Account Statement

Under the manual system, most banks use ledger cards similar to those for checking accounts to maintain records of savings accounts. A few banks mail statements to depositors at stated intervals. In a computerised system, the procedure for reconstructing a savings account is similar to that for checking accounts. In most instances, copies of periodic statements and history reports are available to expedite the process. If not, the account must be reconstructed item by item. Exchange instruments are vehicles by which the bank transfers funds. They are cashier's cheques, bank drafts, traveller's cheques, bank money orders, and certified cheques. Bank exchange instruments are often purchased with currency; therefore, they might be good sources of information about a subject's currency transactions.

Bank Drafts

Bank drafts are prepurchased instruments payable on demand and drawn by or on behalf of the bank itself. It is regarded as cash and cannot be returned or paid. Often, bank drafts are used in international trade.

Cashier's Cheques

These cheques, which are issued by the bank, are called treasurer's cheques when issued by a trust company. They are frequently an excellent lead to other bank accounts, stock, real property, and other assets. Because they can be held indefinitely, subjects sometimes purchase cashier's cheques instead of keeping large amounts of currency on hand. In reconstructing a subject's transactions with cashier's cheques, be sure that all cheques are accounted for because subjects sometimes exchange previously purchased cheques for new ones.

Bank cheques, such as cashier's cheques, can be extremely time consuming and expensive to locate unless one knows the date and number of the cheque. However, if the subject has deposited a bank cheque into his account, or purchased a bank cheque using a cheque from his account, then copies of bank cheques are much easier to obtain because the subject's account records will reveal the date and number of the bank cheque.

Traveller's Cheques

These are cheques issued in predetermined amounts by companies such as the American Express Company, Thomas Cook, and several other banks. Local banks purchase them from issuing companies of banks and then sell them to the public. Traveller's cheques require two signatures of the purchaser—one when purchased and the other when cashed. Traveller's cheques are traced serial number. The issuing company usually keeps records of traveller's cheques sent to it by the selling bank. Traveller's cheques do not expire. The local bank that sold the cheques might keep a copy of the sales order that lists the serial numbers. If the numbers are not available, the issuing bank might be able to supply the information if it is known when the cheques were purchased. Cancelled cheques can be obtained from the issuer. A target can purchase large amounts of traveller's cheques from one bank and place them in another to avoid arousing suspicion by depositing cash.

Bank Money Orders

These are similar to drafts but are for a maximum of $1,000. Like drafts, money orders may be purchased by customers who do not want to carry cash.

Certified Cheques

These are customer's cheques on which "certified" is written or stamped across the front by the bank. This certification is a guarantee that the bank will pay the amount of the cheque. Certified cheques are liabilities of the bank and, when paid, are kept by the bank. These cheques are immediately charged against the customer's account by debit memoranda during certification.

Loans

Loan records can provide important information regarding a subject. With loan records, the collateral that secures them, and the results of (bank) credit investigations, a bank has a wealth of information. When a bank makes a commercial loan to an individual, it requires detailed statements of assets and liabilities from the borrower. The loan file also might include the results of credit inquiries regarding paying habits, loan amounts, and present unpaid balances. A bank credit department generally maintains the following basic records:

The credit or loan file. This file includes the loan application, financial statement, and general economic history of the customer.

The liability ledger. The customer's liability to the bank both at the present time and in the past. These sheets also contain information such as the loan date, note number, amount of the loan, interest rate, due date, and payments.

The collateral file. A complete description of the items pledged as security for loans. Records of such collateral can provide valuable information about a subject's assets. The file should be examined for indications of unusual loans including loans in odd amounts or loans that were not deposited into the subject's bank account. Loans that show unusual repayments should also be traced. Lump-sum payments and odd-amount payments are unusual. Accelerated payments or large pay-downs on the balance might indicate sudden wealth.

Loan records might also reveal collusion between the bank and the subject. For instance, if the records show that a loan repayment is long overdue or the loan has an extended rollover, collusion might exist. Also, loans made in contravention to the bank's normal loan or a loan that appears to be in excess of the individual's ability to repay might suggest a "special relationship" between the bank and the subject.

Loan proceeds might be deposited into hidden accounts, or hidden accounts might be used for loan payments. Loans might be secured by hidden assets or be cosigned by previously unknown cohorts. Alternatively, the subject might have taken out the loan for someone else.

Tracing the ultimate disposition of the proceeds will uncover those leads. Tracing the disposition of loan proceeds is similar to tracing deposit transactions. The proceeds might have been deposited within the bank into the subject's account or someone else's account, or it might be used to purchase a certificate of deposit. The funds might have been sent to the wire transfer department for transmittal to another bank. More commonly, the proceeds will be given to the customer in the form of a bank cheque. The bank should be able to trace the cheque to determine where it was deposited or cashed. The loan proceeds might have been used to finance an asset, the down payment for which came from illegal funds.

Tracing the source of loan payments might provide some leads. As mentioned earlier, the payments might be made from a previously unknown account. Payments might be made by a third party, which might reveal a cohort or a kickback or bribe scheme. The loan application should contain a financial statement, or its equivalent, on which the subject may identify other accounts and assets. The file might also contain tax returns, credit agency reports, and notes of interviews by the loan officer. The security for the loan, if any, might be a hidden asset.

Mortgage Loan Files

Mortgage loan files often contain the most detailed financial statements submitted by the subject. The loan file should identify the lawyer who handled the closing, the homeowner's insurance carrier, and perhaps the real estate broker. The lawyer's files often contain copies of the cashier's cheques used for the down payment, which can identify new accounts. The homeowner's insurance policy might contain a rider that lists the homeowner's valuable assets, such as jewellery or furs, perhaps with appraisals and purchase receipts. The closing attorney will have many of the same materials found in the title company files. The real estate broker might keep copies of personal cheques used for deposits and provide information about other real estate transactions by the subjects. Don't forget to look for accelerated or lump sum payments on the mortgage balance.

Consumer or Instalment Loans

Consumer or instalment loans are granted for consumer goods and payments are blended to include the principal and interest. Computer-generated reports record the loan particulars and payment history.

Credit Cards

Banks are doing increasing business in credit cards. Under bank credit card plans, the cardholder can charge purchases at stores, restaurants, and other places that agree to accept the charges. Under most plans, the cardholder can elect to pay the entire balance in one payment or to pay in instalments under arrangements similar to a loan account. The records of importance to the economic crime investigator are the application for a card and the bank's copies of monthly statements sent to the cardholder. In some banks, copies of the individual charges are also available. The monthly statements and the individual charge documents listing the stores where the cardholder has made purchases can furnish valuable leads about the spending habits of the target. Most banks offering credit card plans are affiliated with a national system such as Visa or MasterCard International.

Bank Collection Department Records

The bank's collection department, which is normally involved in collecting amounts due on instalment contracts and notes, can be used to collect personal cheques (usually in large amounts and with special instructions), thus circumventing the normal recordkeeping associated with checking accounts. Such a transaction will not be reflected on the target's regular checking account statements but will appear in the collection department records. A copy of the cheque will be microfilmed.

Debit Cards and Automated Teller Machines

Debit cards allow access to accounts through POS (point of sale) terminals located at various merchants or through automatic teller machines (ATMs) attached to banks or at other remote locations. Record retrieval is similar as these transactions are recorded on customers' statements and identified by bank specific code. There are, however, no paper documents to support the transaction; reliance is placed instead on the electronic transaction journals.

Safe-Deposit Boxes

Safe deposit boxes are private vault spaces rented by banks to customers. Banks keep no record of safe deposit box contents and rarely know what the boxes contain. The rental contract records identify the renters, the person or people who have access to the boxes, their signatures, and the dates of the original agreements, and later renewals. They also might contain other identifying information, including the name of the initiating bank officer. The officer's name could be significant if the subject (who might have used an alias in renting the box) must be identified.

Records showing access to the boxes vary from bank to bank. They contain the signatures of the people entering the boxes and usually the dates and times of entry. The entry records are filed in box-number order. The frequency of entry and the times and dates of entries might be significant and might correspond to the times and dates of deposits or withdrawals from other accounts or to the purchases and sales of securities or property and in other situations. Of course, proper authorization must be obtained before the bank will turn over any such records.

Stock Brokerage Records

Many stock brokerage houses now offer the same type of services as banks, such as cheque writing privileges, credit cards, loans (against the value of securities held), as well as their normal securities business. All records pertaining to the subject should be requested; however, make sure that the request specifically includes the following:

Application. When a customer opens an account, he will typically fill out an account application that will contain personal and financial data such as bank accounts.

Customer account information. This information is usually computerised and is kept in the broker's files for reference. It will include all transactions conducted for the customer.

Signature card. A signature card should be on file that will show all those authorized to conduct transactions on the account.

Securities receipts. These receipts are issued to a customer when he delivers securities to the broker for sale.

Cash receipts. These receipts are issued to a customer when he delivers currency to the broker.

Confirmation slips. These are issued to a customer to show the type of transaction (buy or sell) and the amount involved in the transaction.

Securities delivered receipt. This receipt is signed by the customer when a securities purchase is delivered to the customer.

Brokerage account statement. This statement is usually issued monthly and provides information on all transactions conducted during the reporting period. It lists all purchases and sales, the name of the security, the number of units, the amount per unit, the total amount of the transaction, the account balance, payments received from the customer, disbursements to the customer, and the securities that are held by the brokerage firm for the customer.

The examiner is primarily interested in the source of the funds used to purchase securities or deposited to a cash account. The subject's monthly account statements, which are somewhat more complex than equivalent bank statements, reflect these transactions. They can be interpreted with the help of explanatory material on the statement or with the assistance of an employee of the firm. Receipts for stock purchases and deposits should reflect whether the payment was in currency or cheque and the code of the bank on which the cheque was drawn. Brokerage cheques issued to the subject from stock sale proceeds also should be examined, as these might be deposited directly to a new account or endorsed over and paid directly to third parties for the purchase of assets.

Tax Returns and Related Documents

Personal tax returns, if available, might provide indirect evidence of illicit payments, such as profits or losses from previously undisclosed business ventures or interest and dividends on hidden CDs and bank accounts. The returns might also reveal deductions and expenses, such as real estate taxes, that can lead to previously unknown funds or assets. Commercial bribes are often reported as consulting fees or other miscellaneous income. The target's accountant and tax preparer should also be interviewed, and their files and work papers subpoenaed, if possible.

Indirect Methods of Tracing Financial Transactions

A subject's income can be established by the direct or indirect approach. The direct approach or the specific-items method of proving income relies on specific transactions, such as sales or expenses to determine income. The indirect approach relies on circumstantial proof of income using such methods as net worth, source and application of funds, and bank deposits.

Almost all individuals and business entities determine income by the specific-items or specific-transactions method. Most entities engaged in legitimate pursuits maintain books and records in which they record transactions as they occur, and their income computations are based upon the total transactions during a given period. In fraud examinations, income can usually be established more readily by the direct approach; for this reason, it should be used whenever possible.

In many fraud schemes, however, a subject's books and records are not made available to the examiner. Therefore, an indirect approach must be taken using the net worth, source and application of funds, or bank deposit methods. Although these methods are circumstantial proof, courts have approved their use in civil and criminal cases on the theory that proof of a subject's unexplained funds or property might establish a prima facie understatement of income.

Elements of Financial Examination Techniques

To examine company books and records for fraud, the fraud examiner must know and understand the environment in which the entity operates; the entity's accounting system (including the types of schemes relevant to the entity and the controls that are designed to prevent fraud), basic concealment methods, and various detection techniques.

The Environment

It is critical to understand the business (or government) environment where the entity operates. To understand the environment, you must have a firm grasp of the nature of the business, the competition, the market share, the financing structure, the vendors (suppliers), major customers, the methods of receipts (i.e., cash or on account) and disbursements, the procurement methods (i.e., whether goods and services are obtained through a bidding process or not), the general economic climate, and the personnel pool available to the entity.

It is through the understanding of the entity as an operating enterprise that you can assess the risks associated with the particular operations. The risks and peculiarities of the entity will help shape the nature of potential fraud schemes that could be perpetrated by the entity's employees.

The Accounting System

Understanding the basic accounting system and its integration with the operations of the business is important. The basic accounting system, including the system of internal controls, is the key element in providing evidence of past, present, and future internal fraud. Internal fraud that is on-book will appear within the entity's financial records. The audit trail might be obscure, but it will exist nonetheless. If the internal fraud is off-book, then other evidence might, with diligent fraud examination techniques, be uncovered. All internal fraud has an impact on the bottom line. However, fraud in small amounts will be harder to detect because of its immaterial amount relative to the financial statements as a whole. If an internal fraud scheme is large enough, it will have an effect on the entity's financial statements.

Various Detection Techniques

Though there are many fraud detection methods, whatever method is employed will usually require the examination of source documents. Many times, these source documents provide the evidence necessary to prove fraud in a court of law. Additionally, in many cases, the source documents will help establish the intent of the fraud offenders. Individual or groups of documents can be examined in several ways to detect possible fraud.

Because most internal fraud is continuous in nature, groups of documents can be analysed for exceptions and trends. Many times a large population must be sampled to determine, with statistical validity, if documents have been altered. Statistical sampling quantifies the risk of arriving at an incorrect conclusion; it is generally necessary with large populations.

Example
Fraud examiners want to examine sales invoices for proper approvals in a company with $2 billion in annual sales. The average sales invoice is $15,000. By selecting a valid statistical sample of sales, the examiners can project the effectiveness of internal controls regarding the approval of the sales invoices, assuming proper interpretation of test results. If deficiencies exist in the controls, then those results should become apparent in the test results.

Statistical Sampling

If an anomaly is found in the financial statements and transactions and further investigation is desired, it might be appropriate to pull a statistical sample. By using statistical sampling, the examiner can look at fewer transactions rather than the entire population.

There are two basic risks associated with statistical sampling—sampling risk and nonsampling risk.

- *Sampling risk* is the probability that the sample is not representative of the population;
- *Nonsampling risk* is the possibility of making the wrong decision. Nonsampling risk cannot be quantified. However, fraud examiners can control it through adequate planning and supervision of audit engagements.

When using statistical sampling, you must draw a random sample. That is, each member of the population must have an equal chance of being selected. There are two primary types of statistical sampling—attribute and discovery.

Sampling for attributes is used by auditors or fraud examiners looking for a deviation occurrence rate (*deviations, errors,* and *exceptions* are synonyms). When performing this type of sampling, you are looking for the presence or absence of a defined condition.

Example

For each sales invoice in the sample, is there a corresponding shipping order? The answer to the question can only be "yes" or "no." If the control condition is that each sales invoice is not recorded until there has been a shipping order attached, then any "no" response for a booked sale would represent an error.

Discovery Sampling

This is the best type of sampling for auditing for fraud because it is sampling until one occurrence is found. Discovery sampling deals with the probability of discovering at least one error in a given sample size if the population error is a certain percentage. This type of sampling is directed toward a specific objective, such as:

"If I believe some kind of error or irregularity might exist in the records, what sample size will I have to audit to have assurance of finding at least one example?"

Example

Discovery sampling is best used when looking for things such as forged cheques or intercompany sales that have been improperly classified as sales to outsiders.

Random Samples

When using the discovery-sampling technique, the selection of samples should be done *randomly*. In order for a sample to be random, each and every member of the population must have an equal opportunity of being selected. Items in the population can be numbered and selected by reference to a random number table. Or if the items in the population already have numbers (such as check numbers or invoice numbers), then a random sample can be selected by using a random number generator from a computer software program. To select a random sample, (1) identify a number for every item in the population; (2) correspond the random numbers with each item in the population; (3) select the route through the random number table; and (4) select the sample.

Additionally, make sure that you consistently follow the pattern picked for corresponding random numbers to items in the population and that you document the random number selection process in the event the sample needs rechecking or additional sample items need to be selected for testing. If the sample is selected randomly and the sample is large enough, then the sample should represent the population.

Documents

Fraud will often be concealed in questionable documents. Missing or altered documents are some of the principal indicators of fraud, and such occurrences should be thoroughly investigated. Certain documents are a natural part of the accounting system. However, when a pattern of these documents occurs, or an unusual quantity of these documents is noted, further examination might be warranted.

The common-sense test should be applied to any document that appears to have questionable features under the circumstances, such as amounts too high or too low; odd names, times, and places; and identical names and addresses. Fraud can often involve questionable journal entries in the records, such as inappropriate charges to expense accounts or inventory. For example, large journal entries in the inventory accounts near the end of the year might point to a cover-up of inventory theft.

An overabundant number of voids might mean that a fraudster is voiding legitimate sales and pocketing the proceeds. Excessive credit memos might also signal the reversal of legitimate sales and the diversion of cash. Too many late charges might indicate that an account receivable is delinquent because it is a fictitious account and, therefore, will never be paid. Stale items on any reconciliation bear watching. For example, stale outstanding checks may indicate attempted concealment of embezzlement losses or diverted cash. Original documents, such as invoices, should be used to authorize transactions because photocopied or duplicate documents can be subject to manipulation and alteration.

Net Worth Methods

Examining for fraud not only involves the examination of the entity's books and records, it might also entail the estimation of the fraud suspect's change in net worth or expenditures. If fraud is suspected, then using either of the net-worth methods might help in establishing evidence of a fraud.

The net worth method (or comparative net-worth analysis) is used to prove illicit income circumstantially by showing that a person's assets or expenditures for a given period exceed that which can be accounted for from known or admitted sources of income. The net-worth method is a reliable method for estimating a person's ill-gotten gains. The method is used extensively by criminal investigators around the world, especially in drug and money laundering cases.

The net-worth method relies on the familiar balance sheet format readily recognisable in the business world and presents a complete financial picture of a subject. It is based on the theory that increases or decreases in a person's net worth during a period, adjusted for living expenses, allow a determination of income.

Net worth can be defined as the difference between assets and liabilities at a particular point in time. By comparing the subject's net worth at the beginning and end of a period, usually a calendar year, the economic crime investigator can determine the increase or decrease in net worth. Adjustments are then made for living expenses to arrive at income. Income includes receipts derived from all sources. Thus, by subtracting funds from known sources (salary, wages, interest, or dividends, for example), funds from unknown or illegal sources can be calculated.

The net-worth method is often used when several of the subject's assets and/or liabilities have changed during the period under examination and when the target's financial records are not available.

An individual's assets, liabilities, and living expenses can be determined from a variety of sources, such as:

- the subject
- Informants or sources
- Real estate record
- Judgment and lien record
- Bankruptcy record
- Motor vehicle record
- Loan applications
- Financial statements
- Accountant's work papers
- Lawsuits and depositions
- Surveillance
- Credit card applications or statements
- Tax returns
- Insurance record
- Child support and divorce records
- Employment applications and salary cheques
- Companions or associates
- Cancelled cheques and deposited items

The question might arise regarding why items that do not change should be included in the net-worth statement, particularly since they have no bearing on the final result. The answer is that a net-worth statement gives a complete financial picture of the subject and therefore should be as complete as possible so that the target will not be able to contest it on the grounds that items were omitted. Additionally, the net-worth statement can be the foundation for examination of the subject, and a complete statement will prove extremely valuable at that time.

There are two basic methods of net worth computation: The *asset method* and the *expenditures* or *sources and applications of funds method*. They are discussed in detail herein.

The *asset method* should be used when the subject has invested illegal funds to accumulate wealth and acquire assets, causing net worth (value of assets over liabilities) to increase from year to year. The *expenditures method* is best used when the subject spends illicit income on consumables (such as travel and entertainment) that would not cause an increase in net worth.

Begin both methods by assembling the financial profile. Identify all major assets and liabilities, sources of income, and major expenses during the relevant period. The increase, if any, in the subject's net worth or the level of expenditures is then compared to the legitimate funds available. Unaccounted funds might be inferred to come from illicit or hidden sources.

The first step is to prepare the *financial/behavioural profile* of the suspect. This is essentially a financial statement with certain modifications and additions that shows what the defendant owns, owes, earns, and spends at any given point or over a period of time. The profile might yield direct evidence of illegal income or hidden assets, or circumstantial evidence thereof, by showing that the suspect's expenditures exceeded known sources of income.

The financial profile will identify most illicit funds that are deposited to accounts or expended in significant amounts. It will not catch relatively small currency transactions, particularly if they were for concealed activities, consumables, or for unusual one-time expenses such as medical bills.

Determine the target's assets, liabilities, income and expenses from the following sources:

- Interviews
- the target
- associates
- documents from financial sources (e.g., accountant, banker)
- bank account record
- mortgage and loan files

- credit card record
- tax returns
- public records
- business filings
- real estate filings
- court records

STEP 1: Identify all significant assets held by the suspect. An asset is cash (on hand) or anything else of value that can be converted into cash.

Cash on hand is coin and currency (bills, coins, Federal Reserve notes) in the subject's possession (on the subject's person, in the subject's residence or other place in a nominee's hands, or in a safe-deposit box). It does not include money in any account with a financial institution. When using the net-worth method, the item that may be the most difficult to verify is the amount of cash on hand, which is usually claimed by defendants to be sufficient to account for all or part of the unknown sources of income. To establish a firm starting net worth, it must be shown that the target had no large cash sums for which he was not given credit. This is usually done by offering evidence that negates the existence of a cash hoard.

Such evidence might include:

- Written or oral admissions of the subject concerning net worth (a signed net-worth statement or an oral statement as to cash on hand)
- Low earnings in preexamination years, as shown by records of former employers and/or tax returns filed by subject
- Net worth, as established by books and records of the subject
- Financial statement presented for credit or other purposes at a time before or during the period under examination (banks, loan companies, and bonding companies are some of the better sources from which to obtain this type of document)
- Bankruptcy before examination periods

- Prior indebtedness, compromise of overdue debts, and avoidance of bankruptcy
- Installment buying
- History of low earnings and expenditures and cheques returned for insufficient funds (a financial history covering members of the subject's family also might be helpful)
- Loss of furniture and business because of financial reasons
- Receipt of some type of public assistance

STEP 2: Identify all significant liabilities. A liability is an obligation (debt) arising from an oral or written promise to pay.

STEP 3: Identify all income sources during the relevant time period. Income includes money or other things of value received in exchange for services or goods. Income is never included as an asset. Loan proceeds are not included as income but are treated as an asset that is offset by a corresponding liability.

STEP 4: Identify all significant expenses incurred during the relevant period. An expense is any payment for consumables, for personal or business reasons, over the relevant time period. Expenses are not included as liabilities.

STEP 5: Analyze the information you have collected by using the following charts.

The Behavioural Profile

The financial profile might give inaccurate or false negative readings unless certain activities are identified. This is done through preparation of the behavioural profile. The behavioural profile might also provide evidence of a possible motive of the crime, such as large debts, as well as additional evidence of illicit funds. For example, if the suspect spent significant amounts of cash and had no corresponding cash withdrawals from his disclosed bank accounts or no admitted sources of cash income, he must have other undisclosed sources of income.

Using the financial/behavioural profile as a guide, request an interview with the suspect. Pin down the suspect's income, assets, and accounts. Otherwise, the subject might invent excuses or prepare false testimony or documentation to account for the unexplained income.

Net-Worth Analysis

Any recipient of funds, whether honest or suspect, has only four ways of disposing of income—save it, buy assets, pay off debts, or spend it. Net worth analysis begins with the completion of a suspect's financial profile. Through identification of the suspect's assets, liabilities, income, and expenses, a net worth statement can be determined. Once completed, changes in the suspect's net worth can be compared to his known income, and differences can be inferred to be from unknown sources.

In computing the comparative net worth, these issues should be considered:

- All assets should be valued at cost, not fair market value. Subsequent appreciation or depreciation of assets is ignored.
- The amount of funds available to the subject from legitimate sources should be estimated or computed generously. The amount of the subject's expenditures, particularly hard-to-document living costs, such as food and entertainment,

should be estimated conservatively to give the subject the benefit of any doubt.

- Always attempt to interview the subject to identify all alleged sources of funds and to negate defences that he might raise later.
- Establish the starting point, generally the year before the target's illegal activities begin. This will be referred to as "year one" in the following computations.
- Compute the target's net worth at the end of year one. Identify all assets held by the subject, valued at cost, including assets acquired earlier, and the amount of current liabilities.

Comparative Net Worth: Expenditures Method

With the expenditures method, a comparison is made between the suspect's known expenditures and known sources of funds during a given period of time. Any excess expenditure must be the result of income from unknown sources. It is closely related to the net worth analysis, accounting variations of the same principle. The expenditures formula is provided below:

Bank Deposits Method

The bank deposits method is a means to prove unknown sources of funds by indirect or circumstantial evidence. Similar to the other indirect approaches, the bank deposits method computes income by showing what happened to a subject's funds. It is based on the theory that if a subject receives money, only two things can be done with it: it can be deposited or it can be spent. By this method, income is proved through an analysis of bank deposits, cancelled cheques, and the subject's currency transactions. Adjustments for non-income items are made to arrive at income. A basic formula for the bank deposits method is

The subject's income is deposited, and the subject's books and records are unavailable, withheld, incomplete, or maintained on a cash basis. Use of the bank deposits method is not limited to these circumstances, however. Even though the target's books and records might appear to be complete and accurate, the method can still be used, and there is no requirement to disprove the accuracy of the books and records.

The basic sources of information for the bank deposits computation are interviews, analyses of the books and records, and analyses of the bank accounts. A thorough interview will determine the subject's expenditures by cash and cheques, identify all bank accounts, and determine all loans and other receipts.

Total Deposits

Total deposits consist not only of amounts deposited to all bank accounts maintained or controlled by the target but also deposits made to accounts in savings and loan companies, investment trusts, brokerage houses, and credit unions. Total deposits also include the accumulation (increase) of cash on hand. Because some subjects have bank accounts in fictitious names or under special titles, such as

"Special Account No. 1," "Trustee Account," or "Trading Account," the investigator should look for this type of account during the investigation. If a subject lists cheques on a deposit ticket and deducts an amount paid to him in cash (split deposit), only the net amount of the deposit should be used in computing total deposits.

Additional items that must be included in deposits are property and notes that the subject received in payment for services. The accepted practice is to consider these items as depositories into which funds have been placed for future use.

Net Deposits

All transfers or exchanges between bank accounts as well as funds that are redeposited are non-income items and are subtracted from total deposits to yield net deposits. Failure to eliminate these items would result in an overstatement of income.

Cash Expenditures

Cash expenditures consist of the total outlay of funds less net bank disbursements. The total outlay of funds includes all payments made by cash or cheque. There is no need to determine which part was paid by cash and which part by cheque. Total outlays include but are not limited to:

- Purchase of capital assets to investments (determined from settlement sheets, invoices, statements, and the like)
- Loan repayments (determined from loan ledgers of banks or other creditors)
- Living expenses (can be determined from the same sources presented in the net worth and expenditures sections)
- Purchases, business expenses (less non-cash items, such as depreciation), rental expenses, and the like Net bank disbursements can be determined by the following formula:

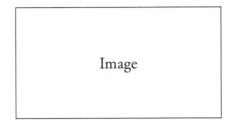

Funds from known sources include, but are not limited to, salaries, business profits, insurance proceeds, gifts received, loans, and inheritances. Funds from known sources are subtracted from total receipts (or income) to arrive at funds from unknown or illegal sources.

Rebutting Defences to the Comparative Net-Worth Analysis

Circumstantial evidence of excess income is often met with the defence that the extra funds came from cash accumulated earlier or from other legitimate sources, such as loans from relatives. To rebut these defences, the fraud examiner must pin down the amount of cash on hand at the beginning of the relevant period (through, for example, amounts listed on financial statements or claimed in interviews) and do the following:

- Obtain a financial history of the target and spouse, through interviews and other means, showing dates and places of employment, salary and bonuses, and any other related income.
- Determine whether the spouse had any separate source of funds that were used to purchase jointly held assets or deposited in joint accounts. If so, the spouse must be included in the financial profile calculations.
- Claims of a prior substantial cash hoard might be rebutted by showing that the target lived carelessly, borrowed money, made instalment purchases, incurred large debts, was delinquent on accounts, had a poor credit rating, or filed

for bankruptcy. Claims that cash came from family or other private loans might be rebutted by showing that the alleged lender was incapable of generating the amounts supposedly lent, the absence of any documentation reflecting the source of the alleged loan (no bank account withdrawals), and the absence of other sources of funds available to the lender.

The net-worth analysis—if records can be obtained—is a significant tool in documenting ill-gotten gains. With this as a basis, the following section covers the major schemes used to commit fraud against companies and governmental agencies.

Locating Hidden Assets

Common Asset Hiding Techniques

In addition to opening hidden bank accounts or purchasing real estate through a straw or front, a target might attempt to preserve his assets by transferring them to other parties or to accounts that might escape detection.

Transfer to Family Members or Parties under Their Control

The most common means of hiding assets, particularly real estate and business interests, is to transfer the asset into the hands of another party that will allow the target to maintain control. In many cases, the target will transfer the asset to a spouse (or another member of the spouse's family), and a husband might make the transfer in his wife's maiden name. Such transfers can be identified through a search of voter registrations, marriage records, and probate in the spouse's maiden name. Transfers to family members can be detected by comparing the target's previous financial statement with the most recent one. Those assets appearing on the oldest statement but not appearing on the most recent statement should be examined closely to determine the nature of the transaction, the purchaser's identity, and the consideration for the sale.

Children's or Family Trust

The defendant in a financial case might seek to protect assets by transferring them to a children's or family trust from a personal estate. These assets would then be protected from judgement or bankruptcy proceedings in a court of law. If the transfer was made to defeat creditors, however, it can be set aside by the court.

Home Mortgage Pay Down

In many cases, subjects seek to hide their assets from seizure by pre-paying a significant portion of their home mortgage. This might allow the subject to shelter his assets in homestead exemption that will survive bankruptcy or other claims against them. By documenting the mortgage prepayment, the fraud examiner can often show undisclosed or hidden income from outside sources.

Example
A cashier's cheque for $96,000 was found to have been used as a prepayment to a home mortgage. By obtaining the front and back of the cashier's cheque, fraud examiners were able to locate another bank account belonging to the defendant.

Insurance Policies

Under the terms of a whole life or universal life insurance policy, the borrower may make additional payments that accrue at a high interest rate and enhance the overall value of the insurance policy.

A sophisticated subject might deposit substantial monies into an existing insurance policy thinking that the fraud examiner will not look beyond the face value of the policy into the equity built up by prepayments. The fraud examiner should, therefore, always examine the financial statement of a target to locate insurance policies and examine the equity in these policies as a potential asset.

Prepaid Credit Cards

Many credit accounts today permit the card holder to prepay their accounts. Many people attempting to hide assets have used the pre-payment option to hide cash from creditors. Prepayment of credit card accounts can also be found in cash management accounts (CMAs) offered by stock brokerage firms.

Savings Bond Purchases

Drug dealers and tax evaders often use savings bond purchases as a means to conceal their ready cash. In several recent cases, defendants in financial crimes have purchased bonds in their individual names, their spouses' names (in their maiden names), or their children's names.

Cashier's Cheques and Traveller's Cheques

Many criminals purchase cashier's cheques and traveller's cheques in an attempt to hide their financial dealings and reduce the amount of cash they have to carry. Through the purchase of cashier's cheques or traveller's cheques in denominations of less than $10,000, the criminal can carry negotiable financial instruments that can be exchanged almost any place in the world.

Computer Databases

To begin a computer-based investigation, contact the county clerk and court clerk to determine which records are available on micro-fiche and which records they provide by computer access. Next, determine how much record checking is necessary, which records should be focused on, and the location of concentration. Areas of concentration might include microfiche records of voter registration, computer access to court records, and real estate files.

Locating Assets through Subpoenas

Criminal and some civil fraud examiners will have subpoena power allowing them to obtain nonpublic records, including bank account and loan records, records from accountants and tax preparers (including income tax returns and related documents), mortgage company records, telephone records, credit card statements, credit reporting company records, hotel and travel records, telex records, overnight package envelopes, and passports.

Locating Assets Offshore

More sophisticated targets might try to hide their assets offshore, often in tax havens and secrecy jurisdictions. Historically, some of the most popular offshore jurisdictions have been Switzerland, the Cayman Islands, the Netherlands Antilles, and Panama. Steps to be taken to locate off-shore assets include:

- Review domestic bank account records for wire transfers or other transactions involving offshore bank accounts.
- Determine whether the subject personally travelled overseas.
- Attempt to locate the subject's travel agency.
- Attempt to identify means employed to move cash off shore by:
  - Use of multiple cashier's cheques
  - Overnight mail envelopes
  - Other methods

After funds have been traced offshore, the next step is to look for transfers back to the United States. A sophisticated target might use a foreign attorney or bank officer as a trustee or front to purchase assets in the United States or appoint the trustee as manager of a US business.

Subjects also might obtain access to their assets offshore by using foreign credit cards. Many international institutions now offer MasterCard or Visa accounts. All account records are maintained in the foreign country. Sophisticated subjects might obtain foreign passports (in a fictitious name, if requested). Some countries offer such passports to people who deposit $25,000 in the state-run financial institution. It may be difficult to obtain information on foreign banks, but it is not impossible. D&B publishes several guides with information about businesses in Latin America, Europe, and other regions of the world.

Also, with the expansion of the Internet as a means of global communication, information on foreign countries and businesses is available through the Internet or through a commercial database or online service.

In his book *Competitor Intelligence*, Leonard Fuld provides a useful chapter on locating information on foreign businesses. He suggests the following resources as starting points:

- Securities brokers with expertise in dealing with foreign businesses
- The International Trade Commission
- International trade shows
- Foreign consulates
- Foreign chambers of commerce
- Foreign magazines and directories

Fuld provides a list of consulates, chambers of commerce, magazines, and directories in his book. Fuld suggests checking *Euromoney 500,* which contains profiles of the world's top 500 banks, or the *Europa World Year Book*, which provides basic data on banks around the world. If the subject engages in a mail-order or retail business, a simple way to get information about his bank accounts is to send him a cheque. Ronald L. Mendell, in his book *How to Do Financial Asset Investigations* suggests buying a small item from the subject by using a cheque. When the cancelled cheque is returned, it will provide the name and possibly the account number of the subject's bank. He suggests that if the subject does not engage in mail-order sales, the same goal may be accomplished by sending the subject a small "refund" cheque.

Legal Assistance in Obtaining Information Regarding Foreign Assets

Law enforcement agencies have some legal resources available to help obtain information from foreign countries. Letters Rogatory are formal requests by the courts of one country to the courts of another country. Mutual Legal Assistance Treaties (MLATs) are agreements between two foreign countries that provide for the exchange of information and documents relating to narcotics, money laundering, and other financial crimes. Some of the countries currently having treaties in force are Anguilla, Antigua and Barbuda, Argentina, Australia, Austria, Bahamas, Barbados, Belize, Belgium, Brazil, British Virgin Islands, Canada, Cayman Islands, Colombia, Cyprus, Czech Republic, Dominica, Egypt, Estonia, European Union, Finland, France, Germany, Greece, Grenada, Hong Kong SAR, Hungary, India, Ireland, Israel, Italy, Jamaica, Japan, Korea, Latvia, Liechtenstein, Lithuania, Luxembourg, Mexico, Montserrat, Morocco, Netherlands, Panama, Philippines, Poland, Romania, Russian Federation, Saint Kitts and Nevis, Saint Lucia, Saint Vincent and the Grenadines, South Africa, Spain, Sweden, Switzerland, Thailand, Trinidad and Tobago, Turks and Caicos Islands, Turkey, United Kingdom, Uruguay, and Venezuela. More countries are being added to the list each year. Some foreign governments, such as Switzerland, will provide information to the United States without a specific agreement on mutual assistance.

Another method of obtaining foreign bank or business records is by obtaining a release and consent form from the defendant. Execution of such a waiver can be compelled by order of a court. However, this procedure is not universally accepted, particularly in Switzerland, the Channel Islands, the Turks and Caicos Islands, or the Cayman Islands.

Letter Rogatory

The information needed for a letter rogatory request generally includes:

- The facts of the case showing at least a reasonable suspicion that the offence under investigation might have been committed
- The names and identifying information of people or entities involved in the matter
- The names and identifying information of witnesses or entities whose names might be on bank records (if accounts are held in other names)
- The names, addresses and other information concerning banks, businesses, or bank account numbers
- The offences being investigated or prosecuted including penalties
- The assistance requested of the foreign country, whether it is documents, testimony, freezing of assets, etc. (If you want a foreign magistrate to question a witness, write out the questions that you want the witness to be asked, even if you ask to be present during the questioning.)
- The procedures to be followed (how to authenticate business documents and records for use in court)

Mutual Legal Assistance Treaties

Requests for foreign assistance under Mutual Legal Assistance Treaties (MLATs) are usually quicker and more efficient than filing letters rogatory. The procedure for making formal requests by MLAT is as follows:

- No court involvement is required.
- The investigator calls the appropriate government agency (such as the Department of Justice) for current guidance and will send a draft request to agency for editing.
- When the request is approved, it is transmitted to the foreign central or competent authority.
- If a translation is required, the requesting agency is responsible for obtaining it.

- The requested country's proper authority determines whether the request meets treaty requirements, and if it does, transmits the request to the appropriate recorder agency for execution.
- The executing authority transmits the evidence through the proper authority to the requesting country.
- The fraud examiner/investigator should inspect the evidence for responsiveness and completeness, as well as certificates of authenticity business records (notify the agency at once of any problems).

Public Records

Of course, a great deal of information that is useful in tracing illicit transactions, particularly real and personal property filings is a matter of public record.

APPENDIX A

Answer to End-of-Book Questions

CHAPTER 1

Note: ❑ T = True ❑ F = False
1. T, F, F, T, T
2. D—individual economic law
3. T, F, T
4. C—when to commit the crime
5. A—financial crimes are not reported to formal response agencies; and difficulty in determining the extent of financial crimes has to do with the conceptual ambiguity surrounding the concept.
6. C—estimates
7. B—White-collar crime as society menace

CHAPTER 2
1. C—there must be a motivating factor for a perpetrator to be willing to commit the offense
2. C—theft
3. D—manipulations
4. D—frauds, fakes, forgery, and theft

CHAPTER 3
1. TRUE
2. TRUE

3. FALSE
4. D—pressures related to needs
5. E—none of the above
6. B—preprepared fraudsters, intermediate fraudsters
7. B—motivational crime
8. B—positioning, intelligence and creativity, ego, coercion, deceit, stress
9. A—social purposes, fair treatment, borrowing, and benign

CHAPTER 4
1. A—witness statements, circumstantial evidence, financial reports on the suspect, physical evidence, documentary evidence, demonstrative evidence, and analytical data.
2. D—observing rights and maintaining staff morale, examination of auditing
3. A—spatial factors, body language, facial expressions, silences, voice, and language.

CHAPTER 5
1. True
2. False
3. C—placement, layering, integration, and investment
4. D—post balance sheet laundering

ABOUT THE AUTHOR

Dr. Kelly Mua Kingsly is a seasoned public finance manager with a wide range of competence that has been sharpened over time to enhance his performance as an exemplary professional. Prior to his presence at the Continental Director for Africa with Nash-holdings, Kelly served as director for Finance Operations of the State of Cameroon, designated representative to the Regional Advisory Commission on Financial Market in Central Africa, cumulatively as project fund manager. He further served as technical adviser in the Ministry of Finance concurrently with his function as adjunct lecturer in the AGENLA Academy on Forensic Accounting, Project Management, and Author. Kelly has enjoyed a rich and varied career spanning multiple countries and disciplines in the international public service, national public service, the private sector, and not-for-profit organizations including setting up many startups for the not for profit organizations.

Kelly served as the assistant resident representative-operations with the United Nations. Under his leadership, he led the change management of the country office, led IPSAS transition for the country office in all represented UN agencies (UNSAS-IPSAS), restructured prerogative for the country office operations, and successfully redressed the program and management business processes.

He has held multiple positions policy and the financial management of the state treasury, which range from auditor, chief of service for cash and accounts, deposits and consignments, computer processing and treatment of accounts, and chief for expenditure respectively. His contributions as a team member and leader led to the systematic production of the first-ever management accounts of the country by his region, a key indicator for admission of the country into the HIPIC initiative.